RAGGED DICK

Neal Bell

BROADWAY PLAY PUBLISHING INC
224 E 62nd St, NY NY 10065-8201
212 772-8334 fax: 212 772-8358
BroadwayPlayPub.com

RAGGED DICK
© Copyright 1990 by Neal Bell

Cover image: an illustration from a newspaper of the time of the Haymarket Bombing in Chicago—the event that triggers the actions in RAGGED DICK

First published by B P P I in August 1998 in *Plays By Neal Bell*
This edition: December 2016
I S B N: 978-0-88145-699-8

Book design: Marie Donovan
Word processing: Microsoft Word
Typographic controls: Adobe InDesign
Typeface: Palatino
Printed and bound in the U S A

RAGGED DICK was premiered by the Immediate
Theater Company in Chicago, on 28 February 1990.
The cast and creative contributors were:

DICK..Richard Wharton
BUNNER .... Brian Shaw
SUSAN .... Peggy Goss
CECIL .... Kris Martin
CLUBBER .... Randy Colburn
AMOS ....John Montana
TOMMY .... Eric Saiet
NORBERT.. Raphy Green
COPY-BOY... William Jones
MRS LANE ....Millie Mcmanus
THE MAN...Michael McNeal
ANNIE ....Lynda Foxman

Director..Jeff Ginsberg
Scenic design.. Tim Morrison
Lighting design ....Ron Greene
Costume design..Frances Maggio
Sound design.. Jeff Webb
Production stage manager ....Robin Gitelman
Technical director......................................Ralph Concepcio
Assistant to the director.............................. Megan Peterson
Fight choreographers.David Woolley & Douglas Mumaw

CHARACTERS & SETTING

DICK, *a reporter*
BUNNER, *a photographer*
SUSAN
CECIL, *an older man,* DICK's *editor*
CLUBBER, *a cop*
AMOS, *an out-of-work stevedore*
TOMMY, AMOS's *twelve-year-old son*
NORBERT, *a chimpanzee (played by an actor)*
COPY BOY, *an urchin*
MRS LANE, DICK's *landlady*
THE MAN
ANNIE, *a comrade of* SUSAN's
STRIKERS, TENEMENT-DWELLERS

New York City

The 1890s

ACT ONE

Scene One

(DICK, *a nattily dressed reporter, and* BUNNER, *his unkempt photographic assistant, are standing in front of a door, in the dark back hall of a tenement house.*)

(BUNNER *is setting a boxy great camera up on a tripod, while* DICK—*excited*—*paces.*)

DICK: I want them to see—the well-to-do swells. In a new way, see. The down-trodden they pass on the street, and it never dawns…

BUNNER: Keep spinnin'. I ain't done yet.

DICK: …that these creatures aren't animals.

BUNNER: No?

DICK: And it never dawns. That they have their own pitiful castles in air. Just like the swell folks'. Except smaller, I guess. And dark nights of the soul—

BUNNER: It could be that they do. But it ain't the same sadness as if.

DICK: As if?

BUNNER: They was human. Smell.

(DICK *takes a big whiff of the tenement air.*)

DICK: Well, it's bad. But it's human.

BUNNER: Sez him. Break it down.

DICK: Fine: onions burning, and piss—

BUNNER: —that you're standin' in, bunky.

(DICK *steps aside.*)

DICK: And cabbage…a lot of bad cabbage, correct?, melting down into glue…some terrible cheesy twang—

BUNNER: Baby-shit.

DICK: Is that baby-shit?

BUNNER: And out here it's all muchly diluted. You oughta imbibe it up close.

DICK: And then under it all…way under it all, down deep, god—what?…something clammy and mean and dark and burnished and why is it making me stiff?

BUNNER: You don't know that aroma? Lift an extremity.

(DICK *smells his armpit.*)

DICK: What?

BUNNER: Fear.

(Pause)

DICK: Do your job, you dumb, shiftless wank. It's late.

BUNNER: Too late. You won't make the edition, Dickie, why consternate?

DICK: Because I don't want to get old on this landing and die.

BUNNER: Without having lived.

DICK: I've lived. I'm an asshole, Bunner, I think. But of a high water.

BUNNER: High or low is fine. I do my job.

(BUNNER *hands* DICK *a frying pan and a starter pistol.*)

BUNNER: The powder's laid out. Shoot into the pan. I'll kick the door.

DICK: I thought you were the photograph man.

BUNNER: I'm kickin' the door. Last time I attempted a flash, the whole place went up. This is not the precisest of sciences, Richard. You just about ready?

(DICK *seems to be frozen.*)

BUNNER: Dick? Could be the light, but your gills are green.

DICK: I'm not afraid.

BUNNER: Oh. Must be my knees I seem to hear knocking.

DICK: My editor thinks I'm down at the docks. Watching the doddering old queen-mother of some place small wash up for a visit. "Stop the presses!"

BUNNER: It's news.

DICK: And this tenement isn't? Maybe it isn't. I write about holes in hell, like this, and that—my editor says—is the page people use to wrap their fish.

BUNNER: So you start to embellish. To get their attention.

DICK: I don't exactly—

BUNNER: No? The O'Hoolihan triplets? Raised by dogs? When found by a horrified social worker, could only bark and lift a hind leg—

DICK: I didn't say they lifted legs—

BUNNER: There was three of 'em, though?

DICK: Don't you think three is sadder?

BUNNER: I seen a lady chewin' on that one. Across from me on the elevated. She lowers the paper, shaking her head. "Raised by dogs?" A tear is running down her cheek. And then we get off, a bum holds out his hand for a single red cent, and she clobbers the gent with her reticule—

DICK: Exactly! Of course she does! And why? Because she can't make the connection—

BUNNER: Which?

DICK: Between the words she reads and the world she sees.

BUNNER: And a picture would hook 'em up?

DICK: Well, wouldn't it? Isn't that why *you're* here?

BUNNER: I like what I catch in the frame, sometimes. The way the light and the dark play off. The rest of it's just a dumb job. You did say you was payin' in cash?

DICK: When you put the wet print in my hand.

BUNNER: Then gimme a count, and I'll shoulder the door, and then count you two more and then fire.

DICK: Splendid. Three…like this?…two…will they wake?

BUNNER: Do I care? Just don't set the flash off till the door is down.

DICK: I'm an asshole, I said. Not an imbecile. "One." Now?

(BUNNER *kicks out at the door.*)

(*As the door crashes open,* BUNNER *steps back to the camera, under the dropcloth, ready to take the shot.*)

(DICK *fires his pistol into the frying pan, with a whump and a clang and then a bright flash of light.*)

(*The whole stage lights up in the frozen suspended glare, and we see a small room—like a closet—jammed up to the eaves with exhausted people—sleeping on cots, on the floor, on boxes, on top of each other.*)

(*Dead center a beautiful woman,* SUSAN, *sits on the only chair. She's dressed in a simple chemise, barefoot, and is thoughtfully smoking a cigarette.*)

(The people sleeping around her are filthy, but SUSAN *is clean.)*

(She stares at DICK, *who's mesmerized.)*

DICK: Wait—

(Then the light of the flash fades out. Men grumble in the sudden dark.)

SLEEPING MAN ONE: Christ Jayzus, McCracken—

SLEEPING MAN TWO: It wudn't me.

SLEEPING MAN ONE: Your farts gonna startle the dead—

SLEEPING MAN TWO: *(Punching* SLEEPING MAN ONE*)* Wudn't me!

SLEEPING MAN ONE: Cut it out!

SLEEPING MAN THREE: You see a bright light?

SLEEPING MAN FOUR: Tommy bent over. The moon come up.

SLEEPING MAN FIVE: GO BACK TO SLEEP!

SUSAN: *(Quietly)* Go back to sleep.

*(*DICK *starts to move to the room.)*

DICK: Wait!—

(But the door is slammed shut in his face.)

*(*BUNNER *comes out from the camera's draping, holding a now-exposed dry-negative plate.)*

BUNNER: I gotta get this in the soup—

DICK: Did you see her?

BUNNER: See who?

DICK: A woman…

BUNNER: I saw the bright end of my nose. And I aimed beyond it. That's all I saw. I'll tell you whatever develops.

(BUNNER *starts to exit,* DICK *grabs him.*)

DICK: I've seen her before.

BUNNER: Did she have a red mole, like a ladybug right at the lip of her cooze?

DICK: Go home.

BUNNER: She's been missing from outa my coop for a month, it could be my flown-off wife.

DICK: It wasn't your wife.

BUNNER: There wasn't no woman in there. *(He exits.)*

(DICK stares at the door. It swings open.)

(No one is inside but SUSAN. She sits and smokes in a pool of light and watches DICK.)

DICK: I've seen you.

SUSAN: Just now.

DICK: Before.

(Pause)

SUSAN: I wasn't here before.

DICK: I've seen you. Where?

SUSAN: That afternoon. This is years ago. Excursioning in the Adirondacks. Indian summer. One last look with your folks.

DICK: They'd take me up, when I was a child. Summers, summer nights, cold...were you there?

(SUSAN shakes her head.)

SUSAN: And they wanted to say goodbye. To the place. You helped them down a steep path, to the foot of a falls.

DICK: They were so thin. I could see right up their sleeves. They moved so slow...And I didn't know how I was like to get them back up—

SUSAN: The trees are on fire, your mother said. Down and around and back and down, in the afternoon haze and the year's last heat, and they walked— remember?—like children, hand in hand, helping each other across the windfalls, leading the way, not paying you much attention at last, recollecting... They rounded a curve in the path below, like that they were gone from sight, and just for a moment you found yourself alone, in the woods. You stopped. You could smell the leaves already fallen starting to rot. Clean, healthy rot. You could feel the heat of the day dying out of the air. You could hear the birds still left, cicadas, trees still moving, the roar of the falls beneath it all. You could taste your own sweat on your lip, you could feel it puddling into your navel, your cock was hard.

DICK: What?

SUSAN: The trees are burning. You could be burning. Your body's a perfect young engine. Blowing off steam. You have all a long life before you. Oh yes—

DICK: And I'm all alone. They turned a corner. Disappeared.

SUSAN: And you think, "I am all alone. I will make myself. An own self. I will build a person the world has never seen."

DICK: And I think—

SUSAN: "—I have never been ever this happy before. In my life. All alone. In a wood."

(Pause)

DICK: Who are you?...Who are you?

SUSAN: I was that afternoon.

(The door starts to swing shut.)

DICK: No, stay—

(The door closes.)

(DICK stares at it. The lights fade to black.)

Scene Two

(The city room of a Park Row paper.)

(DICK is trying to collar his editor, CECIL, who's all steamed up.)

DICK: I wanted to show you a photograph, Cecil—

CECIL: *(Interrupting)* You know what this office needs? Turn around—

(CECIL uses DICK's back for a writing-desk, blue-pencilling copy.)

DICK: Compulsory bathing'd get my vote. Now Cecil, about this picture—

CECIL: You know what is dead-to-rights wrong with this organ? No drunks.

DICK: Well, sir, to be honest, I useta indulge—

CECIL: You did, that's true. Like Sherman had one or two picnics in Georgia.

DICK: And now that I've taken the pledge, there's a couple of others to bobble the torch—

CECIL: Who? Bronson? Fitzpatrick? COPY-BOY!

(A BOY runs on, grabs CECIL's papers and dashes off.)

CECIL: Fitzpatrick's a drinker, Richard. I'd go on record I've seen his right pinky extend. I send Fitzpatrick out today, when I get the astounding news of the Mayor's Commission—

DICK: What news is that?

CECIL: More whores in this city, reports the Commission, than Methodists—

DICK: How do they tell 'em apart?

CECIL: Just an interview's all I ask, with one specimen of the dark sisterhood…and what does Fitzpatrick bring back? *(He holds a piece of paper out.)*

DICK: A poem?

CECIL: And keeping in mind he was gone *all day.*

(DICK reads the poem.)

DICK: "One more unfortunate
Weary of breath,
Rashly importunate
Gone to her death."

CECIL: All day, this was. "I want to move people," he said. "In that case," I replied, "I suggest you become a trolley conductor. You're fired." *He* seemed to be moved. So be it. You mentioned a picture—

DICK: I think it can wait—

CECIL: Time and tide— Let me see it. Now.

(DICK hands CECIL the photograph BUNNER took.)

DICK: It's one of those five-cent lodging houses.

CECIL: Your vasty deeps of knowledge include that this paper's not even set up to do photos?

DICK: I thought you could run an engraving.

CECIL: And what's the point? That twelve sad bohunks sleep stacked up in a room that'd barely accommodate one mill owner's fat girl in a bustle?

DICK: —which occupancy is illegal, yes, and the stench—

CECIL: We might have to fall back on poor words to get that one, God help us all—

DICK: —and look at the dirt. Which they live and breathe—

CECIL: But it won't reproduce.

DICK: —and their shoes. See how—you can tell by the way they don't catch the light now, they aren't leather. They patch 'em up with paper till nothing is left—

CECIL: But it won't reproduce. The dirt is too fine a detail to engrave and the shoes'll look picturesque merely. *(He looks at the picture closer.)* Any animals nursing toddlers off in a corner?

DICK: *(Aggrieved)* Wasn't it *you* who let that story run?

CECIL: Even Homer took a few naps. *(Back to the photo)* Just one little boy, curled up—

DICK: I thought pungent reporting was what you were after.

CECIL: Well, pungent but *true* would be nice.

DICK: *(Of the photo) This* is true.

CECIL: This is yesterday's news.

DICK: But the slums are still there. They get worse.

CECIL: Life tends in a certain direction, don't it? Down a dark hole. You useta indulge as if you knew that, Dick.

DICK: I useta indulge as if nothing meant anything, much. But this picture means something.

CECIL: And so does this memo.

(CECIL produces a piece of paper and hands it to DICK.)

CECIL: Floated down from that Mount Olympus of moral complacency otherwise known as the publisher's office. A referendum's coming up. For the legalizing of parlor houses—

DICK: That blows up every decade, don't it?

CECIL: Our publisher means it to be the last time. Read the poem *he* wrote today.

DICK: *(Reading)*"To whom it may concern: Hound the whores."

CECIL: Man of few words. Or morals. Or thoughts. So the paper will hound some whores. And mobilize public ire to close their shops. And end the plight of the innocent women whose husbands track home to the marital bed the venereal spectre—

DICK: "Venereal spectre?"

CECIL: I never said I was a writer, Dick. I had the dim notion you might be, though.

DICK: Nobody believes what I write.

CECIL: Write better. Photography isn't the answer.

DICK: How do you know? *(Pause)* The world has just gotta keep changin', Cecil. That doesn't mean…

CECIL: What? That I'm left on the shore while the tide pulls out? I'm already here on the sand. With the dinosaur bones.

DICK: *(Pause)* The paper could change. Without you dying.

CECIL: It's already changing, ain't it, Dick? I send my reporters out for facts. And they bring me fictions. Bits of light verse. *Illustrations. (He looks at the photo one more time.)*

CECIL: Who's the woman?

DICK: What woman?

CECIL: The one you musta not noticed, sitting smack dab in the middle and snorting smoke. *(He points the woman out in the picture.)*

DICK: I don't know. I keep thinking I've seen her before.

CECIL: Nice feet.

DICK: Are they?

CECIL: Whereabouts were you looking?

DICK: Her eyes.

CECIL: A woman looked up at me once like this. Like I was the air. She ate me entire and picked her teeth clean with my bones. She whittled me down to my current diminutive size.

DICK: That did it? I thought there was maybe a cloud on your lungs.

CECIL: Who says there ain't? What the fuck is your point?

DICK: *(Taken aback)* I wasn't aware that I had one—

CECIL: Well, neither was I! *(His sudden fury sends him into a coughing fit, which he quickly reins in.)* Except maybe the top of your head.

DICK: Think so?

(CECIL hands the photo back to DICK.)

CECIL: I suggest you go make our smugly intrepid publisher proud. Bring the waste and the horror of merchandized sex to our ken and concern. You can even take pictures, I guess, if you'd like. Somewhere between hard-to-make-out and obscene would be nice. We'll do the slums another day.

(As DICK walks out, dejected, the lights fade to black.)

Scene Three

(A promenade by the Battery. Early morning. A wind is chopping the water up.)

(SUSAN enters, wrapped in a cloak, and looks off. Unnoticed, a uniformed cop named CLUBBER enters, his eye on SUSAN. He watches her as she pulls a paper wrapped-parcel from under her cloak.)

CLUBBER: You don't come down here.

SUSAN: *(Hiding the parcel, not looking around)* Hi, Clubber. That's right. No, I don't.

CLUBBER: You don't come anywhere I don't say. You don't let the waves break at your feet. You don't wash in the spray. You don't breathe the salt air and come clean.

SUSAN: Fine. You see that high queen with the light out there?

CLUBBER: Lady Liberty?

SUSAN: Think you could fill her bronze insides up? Bend her big toes back? You think you could make her drop hold of that torch and go "Oooh!"?

CLUBBER: Have I ever laid one single finger on you?

(SUSAN shakes her head.)

CLUBBER: Then why do you give me such heaps of sad shit?

SUSAN: Just doing my job. *(She sniffs her cloak.)* I don't smell right.

CLUBBER: You never did. You were out last night.

SUSAN: I was? I was.

CLUBBER: What's the news of the day?

SUSAN: I don't know.

CLUBBER: *(Tapping her cloak with his nightstick)* Read the paper.

(SUSAN pulls out the paper-wrapped bundle.)

SUSAN: Somebody died.

CLUBBER: Anybody we know?

SUSAN: My sister's.

CLUBBER: She hurry it on its wee way?

SUSAN: It just come out blue.

CLUBBER: How long ago?

(She doesn't answer.)

CLUBBER: How long ago? *(Pause)* It smells like Limburger cheese. Don't it?

SUSAN: It does.

CLUBBER: That you left in the sun. Don't it smell like cheese?

SUSAN: I said. IT DOES. *(Pause)* Here.

(SUSAN *offers* CLUBBER *the package; he shoves it aside.)*

CLUBBER: No, thanks.

(SUSAN *makes a move to the water,* CLUBBER *grabs her.)*

CLUBBER: Don't throw it in there. That water is clean.

SUSAN: It's a sewer.

CLUBBER: It's cleaner than you.

SUSAN: Clubber? Just beat me, now.

CLUBBER: I never touched one shining strand—

SUSAN: But beat me now. I know you can do it. You have a style. Last week I was watching you take an old Hebrew down. You just folded him up like a pocketknife. And no blood. One bonk. Dancing your club on a string, I thought—last time I saw a club dance like that it was somebody's cock. If you want, I can try to fight back, just a little, say raise my arms, you can smash the small bones of my hands—

CLUBBER: Well, that won't be anywise necessary. Go home.

SUSAN: Home?

CLUBBER: Your room. And don't hoof it, here—

(CLUBBER *hands* SUSAN *a nickel.)*

CLUBBER: —for the trolley. And try to sit down beside somebody proper. And wait till they start to sniff under their hands and then say, "It's my sister's dead child. That nobody wanted, so nobody grieve. That I could have made money enough to bury, last night, on my back. But I left my post—"

(SUSAN *drops the bundle onto the ground and starts to walk off.*)

CLUBBER: Pick it up. Pick it up!

(*She exits. He's livid.*)

CLUBBER: PICK IT UP!

(*The lights fade to black.*)

Scene Four

(*The street outside the tenement house where* DICK *saw* SUSAN.)

(DICK *enters, checks the address on his pad, and looks up at the place.*)

(*As he does so,* CLUBBER *enters across the stage, dragging a bleeding* STRIKER *along, by the collar.*)

(*The* STRIKER'*s unconscious;* CLUBBER *is calm, but he's hot. He stops a moment to wipe his brow; the* STRIKER *lies where* CLUBBER *drops him.*)

DICK: What'd he do?

CLUBBER: He asked me a question.

(DICK *takes a small notebook out and begins to write.*)

CLUBBER: You don't write this down.

DICK: (*As he continues to write*) You know an old sieve, when the wire rusts, and your finger can poke a hole through? That's my memory now.

CLUBBER: You don't want to remember.

DICK: Not you, I don't. At all. Or your snoozing friend. But see how the sun hits the brick over there, at a certain angle, this time of day, and the brick seems lit from within?

CLUBBER: I don't.

DICK: It's over. It's already gone. Which is why I was trying to nail it down.

(CLUBBER *walks over and looks at* DICK's *pad, reading over his shoulder.*)

CLUBBER: *(Reading)* "In the late afternoon, against the incarnadine brick of a tenement wall, the striker's blood goes unnoticed, at first..."

(CLUBBER *stares* DICK *down.*)

CLUBBER: The funny thing being that most of this blood ain't his. You could write that down. A fellow employee—Miss Minnie Garantzig—

DICK: —the sole support of her family—

CLUBBER: —surely, attempted to enter the premises. Where, for her troubles, her scabbing was stopped, by our man, with a two-by-four.

(CLUBBER *pulls the pad from* DICK's *hand.*)

CLUBBER: Do you mind? *(He rips a sheet off and crumples it up.)* Unless you got business down in this dump, which you better not have, I suggest you go on the hell home.

DICK: I'm trying to find a woman—

CLUBBER: Who ain't?

DICK: Would you happen to know who owns this building?

CLUBBER: Andrew Carnegie, wudn't it? *(He grabs the* STRIKER *again, and drags him off.)*

(Lights down.)

Scene Five

(The room where DICK *saw* SUSAN*)*

*(*DICK *stands in the open doorway, looking in.)*

(The room is empty except for AMOS—*who sits in the chair where* SUSAN *sat—sewing a button onto his coat, and* NORBERT, *a chimp [played by an actor], who sits at* AMOS's *feet.)*

*(*AMOS *looks up at* DICK.*)*

AMOS: You seen a small boy, this high, outside?

DICK: I saw a whole gang—

AMOS: With a busted lip and a pail of beer?

DICK: Ten or twelve—they were stomping the piss out of one small tyke—

AMOS: Would you be the police?

DICK: *(Shaking his head)* I'm trying to find a woman—

AMOS: Not me. I got a monkey. *(To* NORBERT*)* Say something. Show us the light of your mind.

*(*NORBERT *doesn't respond.)*

AMOS: I got him from offa this old celestial, pig-tail curlycue down to his ancient inscrutable butt, and he musta could smell him a sucker a good two blocks, 'cause that's how far away I was, walking down to the docks, when I fell in love. So I ask him how much. "You take-ee good care?" I nod. "If you take-ee good care, five buck." "Too much." "Ah no," he says, and he holds this old razor-tipped fingernail up, "but you see—this monkey talk." "I don't give a small fig about that," I snorts, kinda squarin' my shoulders up, "I got me a one-eyed *dog* that can talk. What I

wanta know," I ask him, leaning on in for the kill,
"is—what in hell does he have to *say*?" The old fellah
turns back to Norbert and asks him, "Tell us about
the way of the world." And Norbert looks blank for
a minute and then—he screams. Screams like I never
once heard in my life. And don't hope to again. Like
maybe you shoulda crawled straightaways into your
grave, as soon as your mamma had popped you out,
and saved yourself the commotion. One single short
wavery scream. I gave the old Hindee five dollars
and Norbert hopped onto my shoulder and that was
that. And we're walking along, old Norbert and me,
salutin' the day, and I suddenly stops and I says to
him, "Norbert"—'cause that was my favorite uncle's
name—I says, "Norbert, we're gonna be bestest of pals
very soon, and forever after, following that, but you
gotta just grant me one favor, O K? Don't you ever—by
which I mean never, *ever*—don't scream like that again,
understand?" And Norbert says, "Don't step on my
fucking tail like that old Chink did and I won't."

(Pause)

DICK: He looks hungry.

AMOS: That's craft and guile. He eats more'n me.

(DICK *turns as he hears little* TOMMY *come quavering in, in
his dirty hand a small metal bucket he hands to* AMOS.)

(AMOS *tilts the bucket up to his mouth, preparing to slake
his thirst, and gets only a dribble. Astonished,* AMOS *turns
the pail upside-down, and just a couple of drops fall out.*)

(AMOS *stands and approaches* TOMMY.)

AMOS: Where's my beer?

TOMMY: I fell down.

(AMOS *wallops* TOMMY, *who drops to the floor.* AMOS *drags
him back to his feet.*)

AMOS: Where's my beer?

TOMMY: I fell down!

(AMOS *hits* TOMMY *again and grabs him before he falls.*)

AMOS: Where's my beer?

DICK: Don't hit the boy again.

AMOS: I give him a nickel. He drinks my beer.

DICK: I'm sayin', don't hit him again.

(AMOS *pushes* TOMMY *away, and he falls to the floor.*)

AMOS: Were you after somethin'?

(DICK *hesitates.*)

DICK: I'm trying to find this woman...

(DICK *pulls the photo out and shows it to* AMOS.)

AMOS: Nope.

DICK: I saw her in here last night.

AMOS: Last night?

(DICK *nods.* AMOS *studies the photograph.*)

AMOS: About fifteen people sleep here nights. That's me right there, an' that's Norbert's tail, sticking out of the oven—he likes to sleep where it's warm, though I tell him, "Yer givin' people ideas"...and Tommy's somewhere...

DICK: And there *she* is. I didn't make her up.

AMOS: Did I reckon you did? You seen this lady?

(AMOS *shows the photo to* TOMMY, *who shakes his head.*)

AMOS: We work hard, so we sleep pretty deep.

DICK: Why aren't you working now?

AMOS: I'm laid off. Why aren't you?

(*Pause*)

DICK: How much for the monkey?

AMOS: He ain't for sale.

DICK: Five bucks?

AMOS: Ten.

(DICK *shakes his head and starts to walk off.*)

AMOS: Nine.

DICK: Seven.

AMOS: Done. You a Hebrew?

(DICK *gets bills from his pocketbook and thrusts them at* AMOS, *who hands him the hairy hand of* NORBERT.)

(DICK *and* NORBERT *walk to the door;* NORBERT *calmly accepts a new master.*)

DICK: What does he eat?

AMOS: Whatever you don't. You, if you died in your sleep.

(TOMMY *sadly watches* NORBERT *go.*)

(*The lights fade to black.*)

Scene Six

(*The city room*)

(CECIL *is pacing.*)

CECIL: COPY-BOY!

(*An urchin runs on, grabs* CECIL'*s papers and starts to run off—but* CECIL *snags him.*)

CECIL: Laid eyes on Mr Hunter lately?

BOY: He just got into the elevator.

CECIL: He know the engraver is holding the show for his photo?

BOY: Could be. He was breathing hard. So was the monkey.

(The BOY *begins to exit,* CECIL *grabs him.)*

CECIL: How much do I pay you?

BOY: Nothing.

CECIL: Good. Are you soaking experience up like the fabled and mindless sponge?

BOY: Not so as you'd notice.

CECIL: Why are you here?

BOY: It's warm.

CECIL: It's summer! I was your age, I'd sleep on the steaming street. Who gives a goddamn if it's warm in here?

BOY: It don't stay summer forever.

*(*CECIL *lets go and the* BOY *runs off, almost colliding with* DICK *and* NORBERT, *who enter.)*

CECIL: Got relatives in from the country, Dick?

DICK: Cecil, Norbert. Norbert, Cecil. Don't pet him. *(He holds a bandaged finger up.)*

CECIL: I got the publisher's okey-doke. To run as suggestive a picture as you could bring in. Up to and including bare limbs and lacy undergarments.

DICK: Well, sir—

CECIL: Tell the ape to avert his gaze. Let's look at the goods.

*(*DICK *hands a photograph over.* CECIL *inspects it, puzzled; then he hands it to* NORBERT.*)*

CECIL: Ain't that the same picture he brought before?

*(*NORBERT *scratches his head, uncertain.)*

CECIL: Your cousin the ape and I are a little confused. You were asked to bring in a bordello or two. *This* is a five-cent lodging house.

DICK: —and I know it'd sell a few papers. *(He illustrates with his hand in the air.)* Front page: "Shame of the City. Humans Forced to Live Like Rats. Innocence the First Victim of Over-Crowding. The Face of a Beaten Child." Can you see it? Run this beaut, and in gratitude, Cecil, I'll shoot every brothel in town. Might take a few months...

CECIL: It's the damnedest thing, but I thought our relation was more in the nature of boss and hired hand. I didn't quite get us as equals sitting down at the bargaining table.

(DICK points at details in the photograph.)

DICK: I went back to this room in daylight, Cecil. This man was drunk and waiting for beer he'd sent this little one here to buy. The boy fell down and spilled the beer, and this man lit into him, over and over...

CECIL: I run this, then, and to what effect? So our gentle readers can fleer across their eggcups tomorrow, "I told you those people were animals. Look how they sleep!"

(Pause)

DICK: Do you care what happens?

CECIL: To what?

DICK: Whatever. What happens next. To anything. Do you?

CECIL: Care? *(Pause)* I'm interested.

DICK: No.

CECIL: But I am.

DICK: Not good enough.

CECIL: Dick—

DICK: And I know that you're dying, you son-of-a-bitch.

CECIL: I never cared.

DICK: Are you dying?

(Pause)

CECIL: I had a boy like you.

DICK: I'm aware.

CECIL: You ain't. Because I could say that his hair was a certain color, you see, like grain in light, or he used to run down a high hill so fast it would make my heart to stop, I would think he was gonna fall down and not ever get up, or other he'd fly, just fly away, I could show you a goddam tintype, even, facts, your forte, you'd never guess…how times when you saunter across this room, or your hand flies up to hold onto your beaver, or maybe you pass out dead at your desk and I look at the way your dumb hair grows out…You could just be him. I wish you were. He wasn't once ever an asshole.

DICK: He didn't have time. *(Pause)* I'm sorry.

CECIL: No, no, lash out, it's air itself to you moral Galahads, cruelty…

DICK: I don't mean to be cruel.

CECIL: I know. You don't mean half the things that you do.

(DICK takes the picture back from CECIL.)

DICK: You won't run this picture. You owe me one.

CECIL: For what?

DICK: Because I gave you your wallet back. Give him his wallet, Norbert.

(NORBERT hands CECIL the wallet he's picked from the editor's pocket.)

CECIL: I'm docking you one week's pay. You can go.

DICK: You docked me last week. For the canine kids.

CECIL: Fulfill the assignments I give you, Dick. Or think about moving on to another gazette.

(CECIL *coughs, as the lights fade to black.*)

Scene Seven

(*The roof of the tenement house. Two clotheslines-full of laundry snap in the evening breeze.*)

(*TOMMY stands at one parapet, looking off and idly tossing gravel over the edge.*)

(*Suddenly, SUSAN steps from behind a sheet, sneaks up to TOMMY and taps him on the shoulder.*)

TOMMY: Jeez Louise, you scared me some.

SUSAN: Don't say it, though.

TOMMY: I could care.

(*When TOMMY tries to throw more gravel, SUSAN holds his hand.*)

SUSAN: That hurts the people below.

TOMMY: They don't know it's me.

SUSAN: It still hurts.

(*TOMMY stops.*)

TOMMY: How's your sister?

SUSAN: She went back home…She was sad.

TOMMY: Where in hell is her husband?

SUSAN: Gone.

TOMMY: What'll she do back home?

SUSAN: Work in the mill.

TOMMY: What did she do before?

SUSAN: She worked in the mill. That's why she came here. To get free…

(Pause)

TOMMY: I saw the baby.

SUSAN: I thought you did.

TOMMY: It was blue.

SUSAN: Well, now it's pink. Floatin' on clouds in Heaven.

TOMMY: Oh, sure.

SUSAN: *(Imitating)* Oh, sure…

(SUSAN *and* TOMMY *laugh. He waves at the sky.)*

TOMMY: Hi, Baby…

SUSAN: Stop.

TOMMY: Don't that cloud up there look like a fat baby?

SUSAN: A little.

(Pause)

TOMMY: How come there was so much blood?

SUSAN: It just happens sometimes.

(SUSAN *puts an arm around him and pulls* TOMMY *close.)*

SUSAN: *(Pointing up)* The fat baby's stretchin' out into a dragon. See the tail, and the fire billowin' out?

(TOMMY *watches.)*

TOMMY: The world is turnin'?

SUSAN: That's what they say.

(TOMMY *pulls away from* SUSAN.)

TOMMY: How come, when I jump— *(He jumps.)* —I don't land further down?

SUSAN: Maybe further down's moving too.

(TOMMY *jumps higher.)*

SUSAN: Don't go up there.

TOMMY: Why not? *(He jumps again.)*

SUSAN: That dragon takes a bite, you explode. You ever let loose a balloon?

TOMMY: I want to explode. *(Pause)* I want to explode!

SUSAN: All right, I heard.

(Pause)

TOMMY: Will you come any more? Your sister's gone, you got no reason....

SUSAN: I thought I was here. Ain't I here?

(Pause)

TOMMY: A man bought my monkey.

SUSAN: It wasn't your monkey. *(Pause)* Maybe he woulda bought you.

TOMMY: I wish he had. I get lonesome, now. *(Pause)* He was lookin' for you.

SUSAN: He was?

TOMMY: With a picture.

SUSAN: What did you tell him?

TOMMY: Just like you said—I didn't know you.

(Pause)

SUSAN: You know a cop when you smell one, right?

TOMMY: I guess.

SUSAN: Did he smell like a cop?

TOMMY: *(Shaking his head)* More like somebody who wasn't much good with his hands. Like an office-type. *(Pause)* What did you do?

SUSAN: I saw something I shouldn'ta seen.

TOMMY: What?

(Pause)

SUSAN: Now the dragon's eating his tail. A big smoke ring. Look.

TOMMY: Are you cold? Your hands are buzzin' a little.

SUSAN: I don't get enough sleep, that's all.

TOMMY: You get any?

(SUSAN *pokes* TOMMY.)

TOMMY: Sometimes, it gets that cold in the room, my old man'll stay up and rub my hands. I'll show ya....

(He takes SUSAN'*s hands and starts to chafe them.)*

TOMMY: How does that feel?

SUSAN: It's nice.

(Pause)

TOMMY: Did you ever want babies?

SUSAN: I had a baby. But I was clapped up and the baby was too. And now I can't have any more.

(Pause)

TOMMY: I'm runnin' away.

SUSAN: Where?

*(*TOMMY *doesn't answer, just rubs her hands, as the lights fade out.)*

Scene Eight

*(*DICK *is sneaking into his rooming house, when he's apprehended by old* MRS LANE, *the landlady.)*

MRS LANE: Mister Hunter.

DICK: Yes, ma'am?

MRS LANE: Have I gone mad? —don't rush to respond—have my senses and I parted ways at last, or be so kind as to say if a monkey has taken up residence here. In your room.

DICK: A monkey?

MRS LANE: "A monkey?" My husband smelled like a chimpanzee and I mean no figure of speech. He was circus-folk; I was young; it ended badly. I know the smell of simian much too well.

(To DICK's *dismay,* NORBERT *now enters and stands behind* MRS LANE. *When she moves, the monkey moves—so she never sees him.* DICK *keeps trying—with small hand-gestures—to shoo him away.)*

DICK: *(Stalling)* Perhaps you been only remembering—him—

MRS LANE: No, I think not. When I give myself leave to remember my husband, I see him. Very far off. But I smell no smells.

DICK: *(Vamping)* Nothing at all?

(Pause)

MRS LANE: The lavender water he used on his hair. His hair had a sheen. It was black as asphalt. The dog days made it curl…. *(She realizes she's drifting.)* He had a sharp way of looking through that I for one did not survive. He would have inspected your corpus, sir, and been glad enough to make your acquaintance, and then he'd've turned to me, when we was alone at last, and remarked on what a game bunco-artist you was. Or you *thought* you was. Who are you shooing away?

(Pause)

DICK: Very late at night I get lonely, now.

MRS LANE: Why now?

(Pause)

DICK: I've met a woman. Not even met her. Seen her once…

(DICK *shows* MRS LANE *the photograph.*)

MRS LANE: You took this?

DICK: Nobody believes what I write. I was looking for proof. And I stumbled on her.

MRS LANE: Has it run in your paper?

DICK: My editor killed it. Yesterday's news.

MRS LANE: It's news to *me*. I didn't know people lived like this. Then again, I'm not certain I care… (*She looks closer at the photograph.*) What, may I ask, is her redolence?

DICK: Rain. I don't know…Wind coming up on an empty road…

MRS LANE: As bad as that.

DICK: Very bad. And I must have thought, if the picture ran, someone would come forward. Someone would know her. Tell me whoever she is. And where. I don't know where to look.

(*Pause*)

MRS LANE: I'm sorry for your troubles, sir. But imagine how soon, if I made an allowance for all the heartsickness, my house would become a menagerie. I myself have struggled in darkness not to transmogrify into a batty old lady with birds. Or worse yet, cats. Have you ever sat down in the home of an elderly woman with cats? Like living inside an ammonia bottle—

DICK: The monkey was being beaten, I'm certain.

MRS LANE: Man was born to trouble as sparks fly upward. Animals, sharing the planet with man, fare worse. Sell the monkey or have it destroyed, it makes no matter to me, although—if your options are death or a few quick dollars, I might point out that your rent is a week overdue.

DICK: I've been just a bit pressed—

MRS LANE: Then how lucky you are. For a weekly paycheck. Part of the next which kindly remit to me. And in future, Mister Hunter, please—I must ask you not to cross my threshold again in a like and egregiously vinous state. Good night.

(*As* MRS LANE *exits,* NORBERT *follows her partway out, then turns on his heels and comes back to* DICK, *who takes a coin from his pocket.*)

DICK: Heads I sell all of you. Tails I sell only your fur. (*He flips the coin, inspects it, sighs.*) Norbert, what's this? What's this? (*He tosses the coin, over and over.*) Sparks flying up...

(NORBERT *watches the coin as it glints in the air.*)

(*The lights fade to black.*)

Scene Nine

(DICK *is passed out in a chair in his room, by his hand an empty bottle.*)

(NORBERT *crouches near by.* DICK *dreams.*)

NORBERT: Where can you go? No where. This end of the room, that end of the room, this end of your life, that end. I was hurt. Who helped me? No one helped. I was—why was I hurt? No reason. Stop, think: no reason. None. He just said, he just said, I don't care about you. I don't—where can you go? No where.

(DICK *sits up, startled.*)

DICK: Norbert?

NORBERT: Bite me. Bite me. Bite me. Bite me.

DICK: I knew you could talk!

(DICK *waits for* NORBERT, *who's fallen silent.*)

DICK: Talk!

(*But* NORBERT *is mum.*)

DICK: You aren't the only creature who suffers. Say something, you son of a chimp. (*No response*) Most people have only enough to keep going. Day after day. At work that means nothing. That grinds their bodies to dust. And their souls into ash.

NORBERT: FUCK YOU!

(DICK *is taken aback. Pause*)

DICK: Tell me what he did to you, then.

(NORBERT *is still.*)

DICK: He made you suffer.

NORBERT: OH LET ME EAT YOU.

DICK: What did he do to his child?

NORBERT: YOU DON'T, YOU DON'T CARE!

DICK: I care, but Norbert—

NORBERT: THE WORLD, VAST!

DICK: Not vast so much as complex—

NORBERT: BULLSHIT! Bull—bite me, bite me, beat me raise my hands, I raise —my HANDS!—

DICK: I know they're hands—

NORBERT: Not human hands, but I can still… Not human hands, but pain— Who helped me? No one helped—

DICK: I bought you—

NORBERT: Thank you. Thank you. THANK YOU! THANK YOU! Why did he hurt me? Before you

bought me? Why did I suffer? Why did he suffer? I
bled, he bled, his children bled, his neighbors too, this
end of the room, that end, I was dying, all of us were,
in that room, were going, the women, the men, the
children—away. Going away. Guttering out. All of us
bled. The room was filling with blood, and under the
door, across the landing, down the stairs and onto the
street, the tide come in. Wading a street of blood, this
end of the street, that end, and no one escapes. You
don't escape.

DICK: I never said I did.

NORBERT: You never said, you only thought—

DICK: Most people suffer in ways I can't even imagine.

NORBERT: Why can't you?

DICK: I haven't seen enough.

NORBERT: And if you saw? Could you change a single
thing? *(Pause)* Give away all you have, go live in the
room. Where I used to live. This end of the room, that
end, you eat elsewhere, sixty-five cents a week, go to
work for a sweater, wake in the dark and start work at
daybreak. Work all day in a room like a fiery furnace,
work at a cranky machine in a room with ten others
all bending their backs over cranky machines, and
no talking, and no time out, no lunch, five cents for a
dozen pairs of pants, more if you hurry more, so you
hurry until the work blurs, you slip and the needle
drives into your fingertip, over and over. Over and
over. Over and over. Day after day. Blood and blood.
Move into that room.

(Pause)

DICK: Do you like this room?

NORBERT: TEA COZIES! ANTIMACASSARS! Nice…

DICK: I like this room. Which sad fact means, if I take your babble correctly, I'm lost.

NORBERT: Don't let it detain you. Clutch the moment. Fuck your whore.

(DICK *is astounded at* NORBERT'*s suggestion.*)

DICK: She isn't a whore.

NORBERT: She's a Sunday school teacher. Cert, I almost forgot.

DICK: Is she a whore?

NORBERT: She was when you saw her last. In Chicago. Some lifetimes back.

DICK: When I went to Chicago? Then? At the anarchists' trial?

NORBERT: In court. In the spectator's gallery. Way in back. Most every day.

(DICK *picks the photo up and stares at it.*)

DICK: Great God in Heaven. You're right. It's her.

NORBERT: You used to wonder who she could be.

DICK: She couldn't stop shaking. Remember?

NORBERT: You wanted to—

DICK: What? I wanted to what?

NORBERT: Make her stop shaking. Make her shake worse. I don't know.

DICK: She isn't a whore...

NORBERT: And she has a heart of gold. And a soul. And she isn't diseased. (*He starts to recite.*)
There was a young man from Back Bay
Who thought syphilis just went away.
He believed that a chancre
Was only a canker
That healed in a week and a day.

But now he has "acne vulgaris"
(Or whatever they call it in Paris);
On his skin it has spread
From his feet to his head
And his friends want to know where his hair is.

DICK: Be quiet.

NORBERT: There's more to his terrible plight:
His pupils won't close in the light
His heart is cavorting,
His wife is aborting,
And he squints through his gun-barrel sight.

DICK: Will you SHUT UP?

NORBERT: ARTHRALGIA CUTS INTO HIS SLUMBER,
HIS AORTA'S IN NEED OF A PLUMBER:
BUT NOW HE HAS TABES
AND SABER-SHINNED BABIES,
WHILE OF GUMMAS HE HAS QUITE A NUMBER.

(DICK *swings out wildly, hitting* NORBERT, *who falls to the
floor but keeps on.*)

NORBERT: He's been treated in every known way,
But his spirochetes grow day by day;
He's developed paresis,
Has long talks with Jesus,
And thinks he's the Queen of the May.

(DICK *gets on the floor with* NORBERT *and holds him in his
arms.*)

DICK: You're a better man than I am, Norbert, in every
conceivable way—wiser, braver, cleaner, nobler,
kinder, more moral...but I only point out, for the
record, my friend—I have an opposable thumb.

NORBERT: You must have forgot—so do I.

DICK: She isn't a whore, I don't think.

NORBERT: Who ever is?

(The lights fade to black.)

Scene Ten

(The city-room)

(As CECIL *is staring out the window, a copy* BOY *runs in.)*

BOY: McBurney says, "We're lockin' the damn edition up."

CECIL: Well, tell McBurney to lock it.

BOY: Except they left a hole for the President's message. You have it.

*(*CECIL *pulls a piece of paper out and gives it a glance.)*

CECIL: You want to read the President's message?

BOY: Not much.

CECIL: Me neither. *(He balls the paper up and throws it away.)* Tell 'em the office-cat ate it.

BOY: He ate the President's speech last month.

CECIL: Hungry cuss.

BOY: McBurney'll say, "That leaves a damn hole on page one."

CECIL: Well, tell McBurney I'll send down some damn thing.

(The BOY *runs off. Pause)*

*(*DICK *enters.* CECIL *sees him and then turns back to the window.* DICK *crosses to* CECIL *and looks at the view.)*

DICK: Working late at City Hall.

CECIL: Graft never sleeps.

*(*DICK *hands* CECIL *the photograph.)*

DICK: She's a whore.

(Pause)

(CECIL *stares at the photograph and then at* DICK. *He smiles.*)

CECIL: Why didn't you say so? *(Pause)* COPY BOY!

(The lights fade to black.)

Scene Eleven

(The intersection of Fifth and Broadway)

(Sunday afternoon)

(BUNNER *stands in the empty street with his camera, set on its tripod, preparing to take a photo.*)

(DICK *enters and watches.*)

DICK: Should you stand in the street like that?

BUNNER: I doubt it. So send the film on to the Kodak plant if they mow me down. I want this shot.

DICK: I only see a building….

BUNNER: Just the way all the windows burn in the afternoon sun…

DICK: Where?

BUNNER: You can't catch it from the curb.

(DICK *steps into the street to stand beside* BUNNER.)

DICK: You never called back.

BUNNER: I wasn't within a furlong of a phone.

(DICK *moves in front of the camera.*)

DICK: Look at me, Bunner.

BUNNER: I am.

DICK: Not through that dadblasted box.

(BUNNER *looks up.*)

BUNNER: I'm losin' my light.

DICK: I just came from your studio.

BUNNER: Oh?

DICK: —where I went to pick up all the photos I asked you to take. Of the cathouse parlors.

BUNNER: I liked that assignment, Richard. I truly did.

DICK: And I stood with your half-wit aide-de-camp, in that odd red light, and watched him move the film through the bath, and I waited to see a particular face swim up. And waited. And waited some more. For any face at all to come flooding up out of the dark.

(DICK *pulls from his coat a sheaf of solid black prints, and shows them to* BUNNER.)

DICK: And nothing did.

(BUNNER *gives one photo a look.*)

BUNNER: Not a one. Damn. Well, I guess you don't owe me for these.

DICK: I already paid you.

BUNNER: Huh. Not a single one.

DICK: Shall I send you back? Or is this what'll happen again?

BUNNER: It's just, there's sentiments in the breeze right now I feel like eyeball grit. Crusades. Folks hawking "purity" left and right like some sort of a tangible burglar-alarm for the soul. Smoke rising, Dick. All this talk in the press about how many whores, and where did they come from, and how do we send 'em to Jericho, I start to smell burning meat.

DICK: But I'm not off on a witch-hunt, Bunner.

BUNNER: The good folks never are. And most people are good. It works out, howsomever, that witches fry. (*He pulls a newspaper out of his pocket, opening it to the picture of* SUSAN *he took.)* You wanted a picture, or so you said, to illustrate verminous slum overcrowding—

DICK: I did—

BUNNER: But you used my picture another way. *(He reads the headlines)* "A Night-Walker At Home. The Hearth Corrupted. Innocence Cast Upon Barren Ground. Children Asleep At The Feet Of Venereal Spectre." You useta write moonshine, Dick, which was fine. This is swill. Though "venereal spectre" is nice—

DICK: It ain't mine—

(Just then the policeman CLUBBER *enters again, dragging* ANNIE—*a younger whore*—*by the collar.* ANNIE *is bleeding and dazed.* CLUBBER *stops when he sees the camera, drops* ANNIE *and points his nightstick at* BUNNER.*)*

CLUBBER: You don't want to be aimin' that fucking contraption in this direction, let's hope.

*(*BUNNER *obligingly points the camera off another way.)*

DICK: What'd she do?

CLUBBER: She asked me a question. I know you.

*(*DICK *pulls out his notebook and starts to write.)*

CLUBBER: You don't write this down.

*(*CLUBBER *grabs the notebook from* DICK *and throws it offstage. In response,* DICK *holds up his pen.)*

DICK: Mightier than a sword?

CLUBBER: Don't seem like it is.

DICK: To me, either. *(He throws the pen offstage.)* All right: I'm disarmed. Now tell me what she did.

CLUBBER: She was tryin' to fleece some pitiful workin' stiff. Which isn't sensational news, by the way. "Whore screws over some sucker," that ain't news. "Sucker screws whore," that ain't news either, come to think.

Whores is usual business, only. Which makes it odd, to
me, you could give a rat-fuck.

DICK: Who was the gent she was giving the treatment?
You?

BUNNER: *(Whispered, cautioning)* Dick...

CLUBBER: Am I on the take, is your question.

(Pause)

*(Before the eye can take it in, CLUBBER whips his nightstick
out and cracks DICK hard on the head. DICK falls to the
stage.)*

*(Furtively, BUNNER tries to shift his camera, to get a picture
of DICK sprawled out on the street.)*

*(CLUBBER points his stick at BUNNER again and shakes his
head.)*

CLUBBER: Uhn-uhn-uhn...

(BUNNER stops.)

(CLUBBER leans down to speak to DICK.)

CLUBBER: You ain't as dumb as you look. Which, given
the way you look, don't make you smart. *(He grabs
hold of ANNIE again, by the collar.)* I don't bother these
women much, and they pay for the favor. Of not being
bothered. Tit for tat. Her tit for my tat. It's a market
arrangement. It makes us happy. Exceptin' the times
they forget to supply my demand, like tonight, and I
have to roust somebody's butt. Most nights I take my
cut and they clear maybe ten or twelve dollars a week.
Which is five or six more than they'd make selling
notions at Spenser's Department Store. Why the hell
aren't you writing this down, you ponce? I told you not
to come down this way. I meant it.

*(As CLUBBER drags ANNIE off, BUNNER helps DICK to his
feet and brushes him off.)*

DICK: Was it something I said?

BUNNER: You don't have to be brave on *my* account—

DICK: I'm all right. (*He raps his head with his knuckles.*) Solid granite, my mother liked to say.

BUNNER: You lookin' for news? That gentleman there is an item.

DICK: But not the one my editor wants. (*He picks up the newspaper* BUNNER *dropped, pointing again to the photo of* SUSAN.) This woman knows something.

BUNNER: Most women, it's been my unnerving experience, do. How bad do you want she should catch it for that?

DICK: I only want to tell her story.

BUNNER: Who says her story needs telling?

DICK: Look at her eyes.

BUNNER: Her eyes are as blank as those windows there.

DICK: (*Looking up*) You've lost your light. I'm sorry.

BUNNER: (*Shrugging*) Another day.

(*Pause*)

DICK: (*One last shot*) You never saw her.

BUNNER: Nope. And I doubt I ever will. If you know what I mean.

DICK: Stand idly by if you want to, then. I'll find my missing person on my own.

BUNNER: You couldn't find your hat on your head.

(DICK *throws the black prints at* BUNNER.)

DICK: —says the man who keeps forgetting to open the shutter.

(DICK *exits;* BUNNER *watches him go, then turns his camera back to get the picture he wanted.*)

(A MAN *approaches.)*

MAN: Are you a photographer?

BUNNER: No, I'm the King of Peru.

(Pause)

MAN: I'm Jack the Ripper.

BUNNER: We've missed ya. Huh. You been gone for a while.

MAN: Lying low.

(The MAN *watches* BUNNER *set up his shot.)*

MAN: Is that one of them cast-iron buildings?

BUNNER: I guess at a certain angle it is. But hunker down…

*(*BUNNER *shows the* MAN *where to kneel.)*

BUNNER: And now look up…

MAN: It's the prow of a ship.

BUNNER: A very great ship. And it's tugging the rest of Manhattan up town.

MAN: No traffic on Sunday. *(He looks around)* All the way up. All the way down. Take a picture of me. In the horse-apple straw. In the breakers in front of that ship.

BUNNER: No, thanks.

MAN: Take a picture of deep in my eyes. I was murdered.

BUNNER: You seem pretty lively, considered.

MAN: I'm only a long time dying.

(The MAN *hands* BUNNER *a rumpled newspaper and points at a photo—the one that* BUNNER *took of* SUSAN.)*

MAN: It's not a good likeness.

BUNNER: *(Offended)* This goddess here is the guilty party?

MAN: My throat is slashed from ear to ear, so deep
that the head is practically severed, is how I feel. My
abdomen's opened up to the weather. My breasts have
been sheared. My liver and entrails dangle out.

(Pause)

BUNNER: My wife just give me a rabbit punch and lit
out for the territory.

(The MAN *points at the photo again.)*

MAN: You know her?

BUNNER: This particular houri here?

MAN: I thought you and that other gent was maybe
caught up in this picture, too. You was holding it up...

(The MAN *is making* BUNNER *nervous.)*

BUNNER: *(Thinking fast)* We was takin' a look at it,
that's a fact. That other guy works for the Health
Department, is all. He was worried about the monkey.

MAN: Oh.

BUNNER: We ain't either of us ever seen this woman. In
person, I mean.

MAN: Just as well. If you die a bad death, they tell me,
it burns an image of what you saw last on the back of
your eye. So I figure, this picture's been taken, inside
my bean...and you could snap a photo, close up, of
one of my peepers, and blow it up bigger than life itself
and then there she'd be. Caught in the act of heart-
breaking. Just drain the liquid off and reach in and
pluck her out....

(Pause)

BUNNER: Jack the Ripper, you said?

(Pause)

(The MAN *smiles.)*

MAN: Just havin' some fun. (*He tips his hat and starts to exit, then stops to pick up one of the ruined whorehouse prints.*) What's this?

BUNNER: Somethin' that didn't turn out.

MAN: I thought maybe it was a soul. A shot of a soul. (*Inspecting the ruined photo, he wanders off.*)

(BUNNER *watches the* MAN *go.*)

(*Then, on a hunch, he shifts around his camera and hurriedly takes a shot of the* MAN.)

(*The lights fade to black.*)

Scene Twelve

(ANNIE, *the whore we saw* CLUBBER *dragging along, and* SUSAN *are sitting up in a whorehouse parlor, waiting for trade.* ANNIE's *head is bandaged;* SUSAN *is worried.*)

ANNIE: Has anyone come through the door all night?

SUSAN: Diana and Circe went up at eight. With travelling salesmen *twins.*

ANNIE: How many?

SUSAN: *Twins.* Think. And both of 'em wearing identical suits so loud you could hear them a block away.

(ANNIE *laughs and winces.*)

SUSAN: Take the bandage off.

ANNIE: I was trying for sort of a Turkish bordello effect.

SUSAN: You missed. It looks like you lost all your hair from the pox. Not to mention the dressing is getting dirty.

(ANNIE *begins to unwind the bandage.*)

ANNIE: Tell me how come he don't crack *your* nut.

SUSAN: I always pay.

ANNIE: You've missed a few. It's somethin' else.

SUSAN: He's afraid of me.

ANNIE: Why?

SUSAN: Maybe he thinks I don't care.

(With the bandage off, ANNIE's hair is matted. Some blood is still caked on her forehead.)

SUSAN: Oh, Annie…

ANNIE: Bad?

SUSAN: No. Just a spot, like rust. *(She takes a handkerchief, licks it, and wipes the dried blood away.)*

(Then, for a moment, SUSAN stares at ANNIE. Troubled by something, SUSAN turns away.)

ANNIE: You look like a goose was squatting directly on top of your grave.

SUSAN: Forget it.

ANNIE: What?

(Pause)

SUSAN: I don't know. Like something is after me. Something is closing in…. What if I'm sick?

ANNIE: What you do, you tell him go get it out, and you take it in hand, which raises his hopes, and the price, and the thing itself, and then—when he's got a bone in it—you milk it. See what comes.

SUSAN: No—what if *I'm* sick.

ANNIE: You don't understand me? Why don'tcha? You won't get sick. You take his prick and you skin it up and you pull it down, and firm but gentle, just like that old cow I know you knew, and if gleet starts oozin' outa that thing, you says to him, "Well, much obliged, but I been clapped up now twice already this season, thanks for askin', here's your hat."

SUSAN: But he's clean as an old skin-whistle, say...

ANNIE: Then you lather him up with medical soap—and times I think I don't like the way he fits into his clothes, I soap him up so tight he goes off right there, like—ever seen a dog sneeze, don't know it's coming? K'-CHEW! They look so startled, what the HELL was that?

(Pause)

SUSAN: How do you know I knew a cow?

ANNIE: Didn't you useta lean into old bossy's big warm flank and keep milkin' and go on dreamin'?

SUSAN: Not once. I used to sit next to this reeking animal's steaming butt and hope the flies didn't bite so bad that she'd jam a shitty hoof in the bucket, or kick me again in the tit. This was not a romance.

(Pause)

ANNIE: If you was a man, with a load on, probably, stumbled into this house...and the cheap cigars and flat perfume and Lysol went to your head, and you saw me sitting right here, exactly like this—would you ever want me?

(Pause)

SUSAN: No.

ANNIE: Why *not*?

SUSAN: I wouldn't want either one of us, frankly.

ANNIE: Anyone dares insinuate that you ain't a bitch, I'd be happy to set `em straight.

SUSAN: You look too eager, Annie. And I look dead.

ANNIE: You feelin' sick?

SUSAN: What if I was dying, this minute, all along, and I didn't know?

ANNIE: Well, what if you was.

SUSAN: Well, it wouldn't be fair. Because otherwise, I believe sometimes, I am going to live forever. Truly I think I will. I think I will live so long that I'll end up being everything. Clouds and fields and traffic and buildings and parks and crowds, and ancient. My tits will be as old as London Bridge.

ANNIE: And falling down.

SUSAN: Maybe. Maybe I won't fall apart anymore. Beyond a certain fabulous age.

ANNIE: You'll be lonely.

SUSAN: I'm already lonely.

(Pause)

ANNIE: Did your sister come through?

SUSAN: The baby died.

ANNIE: Good.

SUSAN: That's right.

ANNIE: Who'd want to be born?

SUSAN: You *are* too eager.

ANNIE: Why didn't she lose it?

SUSAN: She couldn't afford it.

ANNIE: *You* could afford it.

SUSAN: She doesn't take money from whores. *(Pause)* This night is a goner. I'm going to bed.

ANNIE: You ain't off-duty—

SUSAN: Tell Ermentrude it's my time of the month.

(SUSAN exits. Unnoticed by ANNIE, DICK enters, hat in hand.)

ANNIE: *(Calling after* SUSAN*)*—which it seems to be more times than the month has weeks.

DICK: Ladies?

ANNIE: *(Turning)* Where?

DICK: This *is*… *(He reads from a card)* "Madame Clafouti's—a Club For Discerning Gents"?

ANNIE: Wonders cease. A live one.

(Trying to place ANNIE, DICK *stares at her.)*

ANNIE: Or maybe not. Can you talk?

DICK: I know you.

ANNIE: All pussycats are gray. At night.

DICK: There was blood on your face—

ANNIE: *(Apprehensive now)* I don't think so, Jack.

DICK: That cop…

ANNIE: I don't know any cops.

DICK: He was dragging you off.

ANNIE: So what?

DICK: He hit me too.

ANNIE: I knew we had something in common. Let's hump.

DICK: I'm sorry, I—I was looking for someone else.

*(*DICK *produces a photo and shows it to* ANNIE.*)*

DICK: I talked to your local apothecary—

ANNIE: The greasy one at the end of the block?

DICK: He said this woman lived somewhere by. He sold her cures for…ladies' complaints.

ANNIE: He also said—to my face, one time—that I was so flat, it'd be like fucking a snake.

DICK: You mean he's prone to misrepresentation.

ANNIE: *(Of the photograph)* I mean that a pound of dog's dinner like that don't work in a decent establishment such as this one. You should try the skin trade by the docks.

DICK: I have. I've been to every ten-dollar palace and five-cent crib on the island.

ANNIE: You gotta be beat.

DICK: I am.

ANNIE: I won't do?

DICK: You would. In a minute, I mean—if I wanted—that.

ANNIE: Then what are you after?

DICK: Some talk. That's all. A question or two.

ANNIE: She ain't here.

(Pause)

DICK: How much do you have to pay off that cop?

ANNIE: Too much. Too often. *(Pause)* Why'd he conk *you*?

DICK: I was watching him doin' his job.

ANNIE: *(Laughing)* You don't wanta do *that*.

(Pause)

DICK: I know you could help me. Won't you?

(Pause)

ANNIE: You could be one of the twisted ones. And how'd I tell?

DICK: Anyone could be one of the twisted ones. You don't work at the safest of trades.

ANNIE: Oh, thanks.

DICK: Is she here?

(Pause)

ANNIE: She's off for the night. Come back tomorrow.

(Then SUSAN *calls, offstage.)*

SUSAN: *(Off)* Annie? My corset laces are all in knots!
Can you give me a hand?

*(*DICK *turns at the sound.)*

DICK: Is that her?

*(*ANNIE *can't answer.)*

SUSAN: *(Off)* Annie! Help! I can't— *(She enters,
undressed, and sees* DICK.*)* —breathe. Who's that?

ANNIE: An easy five dollars.

DICK: *(Mesmerized)* You…

(As DICK *stares at* SUSAN, *the lights fade to black.)*

END OF ACT ONE

ACT TWO

Scene One

(SUSAN's *room in the whorehouse.* SUSAN *and* DICK *come in.*)

(DICK *stares at* SUSAN.)

SUSAN: Hear that "shoosh"?

DICK: I don't. What is it?

SUSAN: The sands of time runnin' down. Best tell me whatever you want. The night is old.

DICK: I've been looking for you. A long time. Do they all say that?

SUSAN: Not all.

DICK: Let me brush your hair.

SUSAN: *(Under her breath)* Oh, lord. One of those...

DICK: I'm sorry?...

SUSAN: Nothing. I mutter. Ignore me. Here. *(She hands him a brush and sits in a chair.)*

(DICK *stands behind* SUSAN *and starts to brush her hair.*)

DICK: You said, "One of those." Like, "Suck a hind-tit—a *hair brusher*".

(SUSAN *laughs.*)

DICK: Are we a species?

SUSAN: You used to brush your mother's hair. Or your sister's hair. Or your grandmaw's hair—

DICK: —in a white frame house all shaded with elms—

SUSAN: —exactly so, and your hand would ride a wave of this paragon's hair, till the ends would spark in the dark, and it whickered the scent of this woman you couldn't have's scalp, and this woman's sweat, and her powder, direct to your brain—

DICK: —where a couple of wires would cross—

SUSAN: —except how would you know? until you was grown and married yourself, and found your wick wouldn't stiffen to dip in the space provided, because—it would rush back all in the dark, the smell of these women you must have loved first, and couldn't touch, and lost, and had to lose…So you leave your unopened but paid-for vestal sleeping, and cat it downtown to my house. And you play with my hair.

(Pause)

DICK: You certainly have us sussed.

SUSAN: I have afternoons off. I have a brain. And this is my life.

(Pause)

DICK: Let's hump and have done, you mean.

SUSAN: I only mean brush your wife's hair. And get what you paid for here. *(She looks up at him.)* Do you want to be staring?

DICK: I'm sorry—

SUSAN: Like this… *(She mimics slack-jawed amazement.)*

DICK: I keep thinkin' I've seen you someplace before.

SUSAN: Your mother invited me over last Sunday for dinner.

DICK: I bet the roast was cold—my mother is dead. I don't have a wife. I didn't grow up in a white frame gingerbread house.

SUSAN: And you never brushed anyone's hair.

(Pause)

DICK: On rare occasions my Aunt Augusta would ask me to rub her old feet. Which I'd do, but wait, now—under duress. Big sweaty red toes, she sold ladies' elastics at Drake's, there was nothing enticing about these piggies, I promise.

(SUSAN *holds out her bare feet.*)

SUSAN: My feet swell up, that time of the monthlies.

DICK: Your feet are as lovely as…hands.

SUSAN: Like a monkey's.

DICK: That's not what I meant. What on earth did I mean? I guess I'm a little embarassed.

SUSAN: I guess you are.

DICK: Not knowing what all to do next.

(Pause)

SUSAN: Why don't you come over behind this Japanese screen…imported at great expense from farthest Yonkers… *(She crosses behind a chest-high tryptich dressing-screen.)*…and let me wash you off.

DICK: All right. *(He starts to take his trousers off.)* I bathed before I came—

SUSAN: —As the bishop said to the actress, I hear. And don't think I'm not grateful. Just let me go back and swab down one corner.

DICK: Cleanliness next to godliness—

SUSAN: Is it? I thought it was next to dirt.

(DICK *goes behind the screen with* SUSAN. *We see their heads and shoulders.*)

DICK: There's a smell like a sawbones' office.

SUSAN: Carbolic soap. *(We hear her splashing about in a china wash-basin.)*

DICK: Do you worry about disease?

SUSAN: I'm not washing you off for my health. Little humor. All right—let's have the thing itself.

(Behind the screen, DICK *fumbles about and produces his member.)*

DICK: You didn't gasp.

SUSAN: No, it's fine.

DICK: I've always had the dim hope, one day, that somebody would gasp.

SUSAN: Faint dead away.

DICK: Something like.

SUSAN: Paint a face on it, then. No, honest, it's perfectly fine. Respectable.

DICK: Small.

SUSAN: I must have seen smaller.

DICK: Somehow I don't feel bucked up.

SUSAN: I'm sure it can get the job done. It does get bigger...?

DICK: What? Yes. Oh, much...I don't mean to say, vast...but bigger certainly. Some...

SUSAN: Let me dry you off. Did the soap suds sting?

DICK: A little bit. Does that mean something?

SUSAN: It's just the flesh is sensitive—

DICK: Weak.

SUSAN: That too. Is this towel too rough?

DICK: Not at all. Aren't I growing by leaps and rubbery bounds? I just wondered...

SUSAN: What?

DICK: Are you trying to bring me off fast?

(SUSAN stops drying him off.)

SUSAN: Some nights are longer than others. Sorry. I even like your face.

(The lights fade to black.)

Scene Two

(DICK and SUSAN have just made love.)

(She sits in a chair, in her dressing gown. He sits beside her, wrapped in a sheet.)

DICK: Things I never knew I wanted—

SUSAN: Quiet, now.

DICK: —I think you just gave me. I never had skin. I mean it has never occurred that I'd want to have skin. I never suspected the skin of this arm, the tip of your breast just brushed it, once, right here in the crook, where it's always just only bent, could be alive...

SUSAN: You must have been ready. To find things out.

DICK: And all the new skin is crawling.

SUSAN: Lovely.

DICK: It wants you to touch it again.

SUSAN: You didn't pay up for the till-dawn night. Sorry.

DICK: *(A question)* I have to go.

SUSAN: Come back tomorrow. I'm always here.

DICK: Not always.

SUSAN: Where else would I be?

DICK: I thought I saw someone like you. In the papers.

SUSAN: The funny-papers. You caught that one?
"Children Asleep at the Feet of Venereal Spectre." The
girls have had some fun with that, they like to call out,
"Oh Miss Spectre?"

DICK: Why were you there? In that terrible room?

SUSAN: My sister had had a baby. I went to help out.

DICK: Go on.

SUSAN: *(Puzzled at his interest)* The baby died. So I had
to stay late. Till my sister had cried herself out and to
sleep. And then finally every other weak tool in that
flat had conked, I had a hope of getting my nerves
unsnarled, I'm sitting there in the dark, in the quiet,
what passes for quiet—a dozen drunkards sawing
wood, I'm smoking along like a dragon, when all of a
sudden kerBLAM, the door's slamming the wall, the
door's slamming, the room fills up with all this light,
like a bomb had gone off— *(She stops suddenly and
stares, as if only now did she recognize what she saw.)* ...
like a bomb gone off... *(She freezes.)*

DICK: Ariadne?

*(DICK kneels beside SUSAN and puts a protective arm
around her; she doesn't seem to notice.)*

SUSAN: All this light...

DICK: Did you see a bomb explode somewhere? When
did you see a bomb?

(No answer.)

DICK: Chicago?

(SUSAN stiffens.)

SUSAN: I've never been to Chicago.

(Pause)

DICK: The room filled up with all this light—

SUSAN: ...like a bomb had gone off...

(Pause)

DICK: Ariadne?

SUSAN: My name's not Ariadne.

DICK: Oh. I thought the madam said—

SUSAN: Ariadne's my name when I'm working.

DICK: Otherwise?

SUSAN: Make one up. Make me up.

DICK: Do we all do that?

SUSAN: Most all. You got to go. I have to keep turnin' em over and out.

DICK: I'll pay for the rest of the night—

SUSAN: Too late. These other gents have reservations. Please...

DICK: I can't get my head clear. I want to keep smelling you—

SUSAN: Well, we were almost to washday, take a sheet home. It oughta be ripe.

DICK: Did you know you were shaking?

SUSAN: Maybe I'm sick. You don't want to run into the bouncer, I promise, his knuckles all drag along the floor—

DICK: We have to talk. About why you're shaking.

SUSAN: Tomorrow—

DICK: —won't cut it. Now. Tonight.

SUSAN: Oh. *(Pause)* Are you a reporter?

DICK: Yes.

SUSAN: Are you the one who broke into my sister's flat and took that picture?

DICK: Yes.

SUSAN: And wrote me down like a cesspool backing up—

DICK: I'm sorry. I wanted to find you.

SUSAN: Is that a fact? And other people want to find me. And now they might know exactly where to look.

DICK: What other people?

SUSAN: A man.

DICK: What man?

(Pause)

SUSAN: You want to stay on the whole night?

DICK: I do…

SUSAN: And pump me.

(Pause)

DICK: Let me hold you the rest of the night. Fall asleep in my arms. Let me watch you sleep.

SUSAN: I don't have to jabber on?

DICK: As long as you're there when I wake. We can talk in the morning.

SUSAN: I could cancel my other tumbles, I guess. I *do* like your face. I wonder why. You have to buy me champagne, if you stay the whole night—it's a rule. And it's thirty dollars a split.

DICK: I barely make that in a week.

SUSAN: Up to you.

DICK: Is it good champagne?

SUSAN: I spilled some on a table, once, and it took the varnish off.

(Pause)

DICK: I'll have a bottle.

SUSAN: Your funeral. *(She goes behind the triptych screen and comes back with a bottle.)* Do you need a glass?

DICK: No. You drink. Let me drink after you.

SUSAN: Shall I show you a trick of my trade? Get down on your knees.

(DICK hesitates.)

SUSAN: I'm going to pour the bubbly down my body.

DICK: Oh, god…

SUSAN: And let you lap it up. Wherever it puddles. Wherever you want.

(DICK drops to his knees in front of SUSAN.)

DICK: I've been with other women…

SUSAN: I know. I could tell.

DICK: …but no woman like you.

SUSAN: I'll give you what you want, you don't have to keep laying it on—

DICK: But this isn't soft soap. I think I've wanted to kneel before you since first I saw you. *(Pause)* Back in Chicago.

SUSAN: I've never been to Chicago.

DICK: All right.

SUSAN: You don't believe me.

DICK: It doesn't matter.

SUSAN: It matters to me. Because someone a very great deal like me *was* in Chicago. Years ago. But that person is dead.

DICK: What happened to her? That she had to die?

SUSAN: She saw something.

DICK: A bomb?

(SUSAN *opens her dressing gown.*)

SUSAN: Are you ready to drink? Are you ready to listen?

DICK: Both.

SUSAN: She saw a bomb explode. Like this.

(*Suddenly,* SUSAN *swings the champagne bottle, bringing it down on* DICK's *head. He collapses onto the floor.*)

SUSAN: You son-of-a-bitch. (*She kicks him.*) You SON-OF-A-BITCH. (*She looks about the room, wildly. Then she runs off.*)

(DICK *lies on the floor, knocked out.*)

(*The lights fade to black.*)

Scene Three

(*The cloakroom of* DICK's *newspaper office.*)

(*A copy* BOY *is asleep on the floor in a corner. He sits up with a start as he hears a commotion outside.*)

BOY: What the hell…

ANNIE: (*Off*) Easy does it, don't drop him, Christ—

THE JOHN: (*Off*) Well where's his fuckin' manners, then, he just lost a spaghetti dinner all over my leg—

(*Offstage,* DICK *groans.*)

(*Frightened, the* BOY *runs off.*)

BOY: (*Exiting*) Mister Whilom! Oh, Mister Whilom! Help!

(*As the* BOY *exits,* DICK *is dragged in from the opposite side, supported by* ANNIE *and one of* ANNIE's *customers. Both* THE JOHN *and* ANNIE *are dressed for a masquerade ball, she with a simple domino-mask pushed onto her forehead, and he with a skull-like mask pushed up on his head.)*

ANNIE: Is this the right office?

THE JOHN: Don't know, don't care. Just dump yer load, let me find a wash basin, clean these brand-new trouser-pants, we're late. I don't want to miss out on the band.

(THE JOHN exits, leaving ANNIE to prop DICK up alone.)

(DICK sways; ANNIE struggles to hold him up.)

DICK: I've died a bad death and gone to hell.

ANNIE: What's it like?

DICK: Like the office cloakroom. I'd never have guessed.

ANNIE: No offense, but I'm hours late for a dance already. You think you can stand alone?

DICK: I've been forced to. Times too numerous. Step aside…

(ANNIE lets go of DICK, who sways and then stands his ground. At that moment CECIL runs in, the copy BOY close behind.)

CECIL: Now what's all this?

DICK: Cecil! You ended up down here too?

(DICK turns to greet CECIL, sways and goes down like a sack of potatoes.)

(ANNIE kneels beside DICK and helps him sit up.)

CECIL: Somebody tell me what's happening! NOW!

ANNIE: He was hit.

CECIL: Hit where?

ANNIE: In the whorehouse.

(CECIL turns to the copy BOY.)

CECIL: Go get my bottle.

BOY: You have a bottle?

CECIL: I've seen your grubby, small paw-prints on it.
Run extremely fast.

(The copy BOY runs off.)

CECIL: Doin' research, Dick?

DICK: I found her, Cecil.

CECIL: Found who?

DICK: The woman. The one who saw.

CECIL: Saw what?

(DICK doesn't answer. CECIL turns to ANNIE.)

CECIL: You know what in hell and damnation he's
talking about?

ANNIE: No, sir. I'm a simple working girl.

CECIL: You must have given him quite a ride.

ANNIE: This wasn't my doin'. I'm better than that. This
was one of the nervy ones. Cold-cocked him with a
bottle of vino. Left it to me and my friend to clean up.

CECIL: You could've just shoveled him into the gutter.

ANNIE: Madame Clafouti don't think it looks right—a
row of bodies outside the door.

*(ANNIE stands, gently moving away from DICK, who
continues to sit on the floor.)*

ANNIE: Did you happen to see my beau? Bony gent
with a cape?

CECIL: I didn't.

ANNIE: *(Calling)* Walter?

*(ANNIE exits. DICK pulls a wrinkled and dog-eared
photograph out of his pocket.)*

CECIL: What's that?

DICK: It's the very first picture I took of her. *(Pause)* I found her, Cecil. And then I lost her. *(He wants to get up and gets as far as his hands and knees.)* Ah, Jesus…

CECIL: Take your time. You don't have to stand. Sometimes I think standing is overrated.

DICK: I lost her, Cecil.

CECIL: I know the feeling.

DICK: You don't.

CECIL: No, I do. I seem to lose whole days, these days. They go somewhere. And don't come back. *(Pause)* Like now.

DICK: Now?

CECIL: I was dining alone at Delmonico's. Bliss. It was seven o'clock. And now it's twelve. I've lost five hours. Completely.

DICK: I mislaid a whole year one year.

CECIL: But at least you had fun in the process of losing it.

DICK: Did I?

(The copy BOY *runs up with a bottle of whisky and holds it out to* CECIL.*)*

CECIL: What's this?

BOY: You wanted your bottle.

CECIL: *(Bluffing)* Of course I did.

*(*DICK *reaches up for the bottle.)*

DICK: I could use a medicinal nip.

*(*CECIL *snatches the bottle away.)*

CECIL: No, you couldn't. *(To the* BOY*)* Track down that whore and her dinner ticket, and give 'em the boot off the premises.

(The BOY *runs off.)*

DICK: Just hand the bottle over, you ancient fart.

CECIL: I need you sober. Now more than ever. The purity movement's picking up steam, you can shovel the coal of your moral indignation into the fire, the paper can ride this juggernaut on to the end of the line, the vote on legalization's a deafening NO, and I get to go out in a thunder of sparks.

DICK: And the houses close down. And she's out on the street. And what if somebody is waiting.

CECIL: Waiting?

DICK: To hurt her.

CECIL: Find her first.

DICK: *(Regarding the photo)* I don't know how.

(CECIL *takes the photo from* DICK *and gives it a look.)*

CECIL: Try askin' the boy.

DICK: I did. He said he don't know her.

CECIL: I guess he was lying, then, Richard. Looks to me like he loves her.

DICK: What are you talking about? He's asleep.

(CECIL *hands the photo back.)*

CECIL: Look again. He's got one eye cocked. He's watching that whore like a baby chick watches its momma. Like she was the air he breathed. I know that look....

DICK: I'd swear his eyes were shut, before. But one of 'em's open, now.

CECIL: *(Confused)* One what?

DICK: You fadin' out, Cecil?

CECIL: Am I? *(He looks around, confused.)* Oh, god, it gets dark, and I...

DICK: What?

CECIL: It gets dark, and I don't know where I am.

(DICK *struggles unsteadily onto his feet and puts an arm around* CECIL.)

CECIL: I thought I was sound asleep. I don't sleep in the cloakroom, do I?

DICK: Hold on, old son. It's late, you're tired, that's all.

(THE JOHN *and* ANNIE *reenter.* THE JOHN's *skull-mask is down on his face. Impatient, he moves for the door, while* ANNIE *comes down to speak to* DICK.)

ANNIE: Think you'll live?

DICK: I'm afraid I might.

CECIL: (*Whispered, to* DICK) Who's she?

ANNIE: Come by some night, I'll show you who I am. You can give me a turn.

CECIL: No, I couldn't. You'd lie there, madam, odalisque-like, I'd start an approach…and the next I knew I'd be buttoning up my trousers. Wondering why they were open.

ANNIE: I'm better than *that*.

(CECIL *shakes his head.*)

ANNIE: Well, suit your old self.

(THE JOHN *calls out to* ANNIE.)

THE JOHN: You ready?

(*For the first time,* CECIL *sees the deathlike apparition.*)

CECIL: No. I won't ever be ready. Why are you wearing a cape?

THE JOHN: Ain't it swell?

CECIL: Yes. Open it up. Let me see all the rest of your bones.

(THE JOHN *joins* ANNIE *and gives her a questioning look.*)

THE JOHN: (*Of* CECIL) Moonstruck?

ANNIE: Old. Just old.

(ANNIE *and* THE JOHN *start to move off; then* ANNIE *stops, pulls something out of her bag, and comes back.*)

ANNIE: I almost forgot. You musta dropped this when you dropped your pants.

(ANNIE *hands* DICK *his notepad. Then she takes* THE JOHN's *arm and they exit.* DICK *opens the pad.*)

CECIL: Dick?

DICK: What?

CECIL: He was here.

DICK: Who?

(CECIL *doesn't respond.*)

DICK: Who, Cecil?

CECIL: Death. In a cape.

(*Pause*)

DICK: You think that was death in a cape?

CECIL: It wasn't. Was it?

DICK: No.

CECIL: I'm afraid.

DICK: I'm sorry.

CECIL: Don't leave me, then—

DICK: I never said—

CECIL: You don't have to say. You're runnin' down a high hill, so fast...I'm always left behind. (*Pause*) But don't leave me, Dick. Be my standard-bearer. Write what I ask you to write.

DICK: I have.

(DICK *shows* CECIL *the pad.* CECIL *reads.*)

CECIL: "What more distressing picture than this—a young wife of a few weeks, innocent of that baser nature in man which has led her husband, before the wedding day, to pollute his soul and body in some rank bed of shame...a young wife forced to consult a physician, who tells her that she has become the newest victim of the venereal spectre..." (*To* DICK) "Venereal spectre" is nice....

DICK: I stole it.

(DICK *reaches across, tears off the sheet that* CECIL *was reading.*)

(*Pause*)

CECIL: Do you think you'll remember me? Ten years from now?

(DICK *doesn't answer.*)

CECIL: When my mother was old—much older than I am now—she used to say, "My soul can fly wherever it has to. But where will my memory go, do I have to lose that?"

DICK: But that's just it. My whore knows something that everyone else has forgotten. She wants to fade away. I have to stop her.

CECIL: Find her, then. Save her memory up. Write her story. Only don't be fond of her, even a little.

DICK: No?

CECIL: Is she clean?

DICK: I don't know. I don't care.

CECIL: And what do you think I'm dying of, Richard—old age?

(DICK *stares at* CECIL.)

(*The copy* BOY *reenters and lies back down in his corner.*)

BOY: Assumin' you gents wouldn't mind...I was tryin' to sleep.

CECIL: That tad over there...

DICK: What about him.

CECIL: It's not my son....

(Pause)

DICK: It's not. It's the copy-boy.

(Pause)

CECIL: Do what you want. Fall in love with her. Fuck her. Die a slow death. Only give me that piece you wrote. *(He holds his hand out.)*

DICK: You don't need this, Cecil. It's horse manure. You write better copy yourself.

CECIL: But you wrote it. You wrote it to help me. I want to print something *you* wrote.

DICK: I can't. I'm sorry. *(He crumples up the story.)*

(Pause)

CECIL: You understand you're fired.

DICK: It's worse than that. I quit. *(He starts to exit.)*

(Still woozy, he stumbles and sinks to one knee.)

(CECIL only stares and doesn't move to help him.)

(By himself DICK stands and regains his balance.)

CECIL: I don't care, but where will you go?

DICK: I have to find the boy.

(DICK exits, as CECIL watches.)

(The lights fade to black.)

Scene Four

(Central Park, by the Lake.)

(Night)

(Across the water a band is playing.)

(Nervously, SUSAN paces the shore of the lake, dressed in a traveling cloak and bonnet. She looks around as she hears a crashing sound.)

SUSAN: Who's there?

TOMMY: *(Off)* No goddamn body but me. *(He appears, his clothes more tattered than ever, twigs in his hair.)*

SUSAN: I told your old man ten o'clock. It's one.

TOMMY: You also told him, "meet by the lake." And that's like, "Say, you're from New York City? Know a tall guy named Pete?" Jeez. This lake's a monster....

SUSAN: I thought you'd come on to this cove. My fault. We sat on that mossy rock, one time, and ate peach ice-cream.

TOMMY: How old was I?

SUSAN: *(Pause)* Not old. You wouldn't remember.

TOMMY: Was my mother a whore?

SUSAN: No.

TOMMY: But was she?

SUSAN: She took in laundry. Times the rent was due, and your father had drunk it all up, she'd go out.

TOMMY: Maybe he ain't my old man.

SUSAN: It's a poser.

TOMMY: Maybe he ain't. Hot dog.

(SUSAN puts an arm around him.)

TOMMY: They look at the lake. I thought they was fireflies.

SUSAN: What?

TOMMY: *(Pointing)* The lights on the boats. That other time. I remember the peach ice cream. You said, if those was fireflies, they'd be as big as trolley cars. And I thought you meant they was as big. So I started to cry.

SUSAN: You did, that's right. And we never could figure your problem.

(Pause)

TOMMY: You're goin' away.

SUSAN: I have to.

TOMMY: Go.

SUSAN: So I wanted to say goodbye.

(Pause)

TOMMY: What did you see so bad? You said you saw something you shouldn'ta seen—

SUSAN: Just never mind.

TOMMY: Are you going away? You are. Are you leaving me here? I guess. I get to know why. That's fair.

SUSAN: Nothing is fair. *(Pause)* I saw some men get hanged.

TOMMY: For what?

SUSAN: For nothing. For throwing a bomb they never threw.

TOMMY: Where?

SUSAN: At a workers' rally. *(Pause)* A bomb went off. Some cops were killed.

TOMMY: Were you there?

(SUSAN *doesn't answer. It dawns on* TOMMY.)

TOMMY: You saw....

SUSAN: *(Denying)* I told you what I saw. Four men in the air. And their hands and their legs were tied. And they jerked like fish.

TOMMY: But they fell for somebody else. *(Pause)* Tell me who.

SUSAN: And sink the both of us deep in the shit. No thanks. I like you some more than that.

TOMMY: A lot more?

SUSAN: A man is onto me now. So I have to go find a hole someplace. And then pull the hole in behind me.

TOMMY: Where?

SUSAN: Don't ask me where.

TOMMY: Here in the city?

(SUSAN *doesn't answer.*)

TOMMY: Tell me who threw the bomb.

SUSAN: I won't.

TOMMY: I always wanted to fuck you.

(*Hurt and frantic,* SUSAN *slaps* TOMMY. *He starts to cry, but not like a baby.*)

TOMMY: I always did.

(*Regretful,* SUSAN *pulls* TOMMY *to her and strokes his head while he cries.*)

(*Finally, he pulls away.*)

TOMMY: I meant that like a compliment.

SUSAN: Why do I doubt that, friend-o-mine? You wanted to cut me up, and you did. But I wish I had left you unslapped.

TOMMY: Didn't hurt.

SUSAN: You want I should do it again?

(TOMMY *touches* SUSAN's *face. She starts to move his hand away, then stops herself. He traces her face, committing the feel to memory.*)

(*Then he suddenly runs away and is gone. Startled by his disappearance,* SUSAN *stands alone by the lake.* CLUBBER *enters. She hides her surprise.*)

CLUBBER: Throwin' another kid away?

SUSAN: He's not a kid.

CLUBBER: Spent too much idle time at your dimpled knee.

SUSAN: He said he wanted to fuck me.

CLUBBER: Stand in line.

(SUSAN *starts to exit,* CLUBBER *grabs her.*)

CLUBBER: You don't go anywhere.

SUSAN: I'm meetin' a train.

CLUBBER: Meeting? Or taking?

(*Pause*)

SUSAN: Were you following me?

CLUBBER: I saw you scramblin' out of the house. I decided to tag along.

SUSAN: I need a place to hide.

CLUBBER: Do I wanta know why?

SUSAN: I just have to be gone for awhile.

CLUBBER: All right. (*He starts to unbutton his tunic.*) Climb on inside.

SUSAN: I can't hide in you.

CLUBBER: There ain't no other where. (*He continues undressing.*)

SUSAN: What are you doing?

CLUBBER: I thought I was easing my mind.

SUSAN: Right here in the park.

CLUBBER: Aren't I the full force of the law? *(Pause)*

(As CLUBBER *and* SUSAN *talk he undresses, until he's down to his union suit.)*

CLUBBER: Get out of those travelling duds.

SUSAN: Will you help me escape?

CLUBBER: Depends on how this goes. *(Pause)*

*(*SUSAN *drops her cloak and starts to undress.)*

SUSAN: Who lets you live? You took my money, a couple of years, you let me live. And who allows you?

CLUBBER: You do. You all do. You put up. *(He continues to strip.)* This particular suit of clothes I was wearing the night I first rousted you, Susan. How about that? And you wrapped your powdery arms around me and told me, all in the line of professional duty, you loved me. I never been able to get the scent out.

SUSAN: You put on weight. It's too bad.

CLUBBER: Is it? You useta fancy me, did you?

SUSAN: I liked your eyes. Something buried way deep inside. A small light.

*(*SUSAN *steps out of her dress. In corset and bloomers, she crosses to* CLUBBER, *and stares at his face.)*

CLUBBER: Still there? Anywhere?

SUSAN: *(Shaking her head)* It's gone out.

(Pause)

*(*CLUBBER *moves away and picks up* SUSAN *purse.)*

SUSAN: What are you doing?

*(*CLUBBER *pulls a large wad of bills from* SUSAN's *purse.)*

CLUBBER: I thought the wages of sin was death.

SUSAN: No. It's five dollars a pop.

CLUBBER: How many hundreds of shots in the dark is this?

SUSAN: It's all I saved. In seven years.

CLUBBER: 'Bye, Susan. *(He starts to exit, dressed in his union suit.)*

SUSAN: Where are you going?

CLUBBER: Swimming.

SUSAN: Give me my money.

CLUBBER: It's fish-food, Susan.

SUSAN: I thought you wanted to—

CLUBBER: What? *(Pause)* When you were starin' into my eyes, I was looking in yours.

SUSAN: What did you see?

CLUBBER: The dark. Like mine. But worse.

SUSAN: How?

CLUBBER: You *smiling* in the dark. Like you were at home.

(Pause)

SUSAN: I'm cold.

CLUBBER: The water is warmer than air, this time of night. *(He moves to exit.)*

SUSAN: Hold me.

CLUBBER: I would. But you wouldn't know how to hold me.

(CLUBBER exits. SUSAN watches, putting her dress back on.)

SUSAN: Get out of the water!

CLUBBER: *(Off)* I do this all the time, in the summer. Float out on my back. Look up at the stars.

SUSAN: I WANT MY MONEY!

CLUBBER: *(Off)* Dive in. I think some of it hasn't sunk, yet.

(Pause)

SUSAN: I don't allow you! I can't even vote! You can't just steal my money!

CLUBBER: *(Off)* Call a cop!

(Pause)

(SUSAN, her clothes in a state of disarray, looks off at the lake.)

(The lights fade to black.)

Scene Five

(The dark hall outside the tenement room where DICK saw SUSAN.)

(DICK enters, slightly drunk, on tiptoe, followed by NORBERT. He turns to the monkey, a fingertip pressed to his lips.)

DICK: Shhh…

(This cracks DICK up, for a moment, and then—under NORBERT's stare—he sobers up.)

DICK: Right. *(He raps very hard on the door. To NORBERT, pronouncing the words in English)* No respondez-vous. *(He knocks again.)*

AMOS: *(Off)* We're out!

DICK: *(To NORBERT)* They're OUT. *(He knocks again.)*

AMOS: *(Off)* Completely out.

DICK: Time for a strategem, Norbert. Hrem… *(He orates.)*
"The golf links are so near the mill

that almost every day,
the laboring children can look out
and see the men at play."

(Pause)

(The door opens a crack.)

(AMOS sticks his head out. He's very drunk.)

AMOS: Did you write that?

DICK: I'm a writer.

AMOS: That poem?

DICK: THE GOLF LINKS ARE SO NEAR THE MILL

AMOS: THAT ALMOST EVERY DAY

DICK: THE LABORING CHILDREN CAN LOOK OUT

AMOS: AND SEE THE MEN AT PLAY. *(He steps into the hallway, shutting the door behind him.)* I like that poem. You wrote it.

DICK: A fallen comrade name of Fitzpatrick wrote the words. I wrote the silence *around* the words. I wrote the way I stand in the piss and the swill you call beer in this hall and recite a few maudlin lines about kiddies oppressed and the men at play…and nobody hears.

AMOS: I heard.

(AMOS, blind drunk, sinks onto his knees with a thud. The door opens, and TOMMY looks out.)

TOMMY: Get up.

DICK: He's a little glorious, maybe.

TOMMY: Get up!

(Pause)

DICK: How much for the boy?

AMOS: He ain't for sale.

(DICK hauls a wallet out and starts peeling off bills.)

DICK: Fifteen.

AMOS: The boy's a pearl. Without a price. Just take him.

TOMMY: No.

AMOS: Just TAKE HIM.

TOMMY: GET UP!

(DICK *sizes the situation up.*)

DICK: *(To* TOMMY*)* Do you know where she is?

(TOMMY *won't answer.*)

DICK: Say "no."

TOMMY: No.

DICK: You lie through your badly kept teeth. Which shows to go you how far I've come. I can just about tell. Where is she?

AMOS: Who?

TOMMY: That whore, he means.

AMOS: Susan? The one that wanted to meet you, to say goodbye?

(TOMMY *glares at* AMOS.*)*

DICK: Her name is Susan? *(Pause)* Did you meet her?

(No answer)

DICK: Say "no."

TOMMY: No.

DICK: She was cutting her losses. Big, messy, recalcitrant ones like myself. And runty, quick losses like you.

TOMMY: It was god-mother-fucking-damn *you* she was running away from!

(Pause)

DICK: Let me just fade away, she said.

TOMMY: She did not.

DICK: She kissed your whiskerless cheek.

TOMMY: Not once.

DICK: You touched her face.

TOMMY: You don't know.

DICK: I do. I'd have wanted to touch her face... And then, when she thought she was finally rid of your rubbish, she walked across town, or up or down, to her newest digs. And you trailed her. All along in the dark. Like a dog. Right? Say, "No, I didn't."

TOMMY: NO!

(Pause)

DICK: Will you take me there? I'm not the one she's running away from. I'm the one that can save her.

TOMMY: How?

DICK: I get her story out to the world. Then no one can move against her, in all the glare.

(TOMMY looks to AMOS.)

TOMMY: Old man?

AMOS: I thought I had always three choices, sir. Rise, until I was in a fair place to oppress my fellows, or fall, into crime, and grow fat that way. Or else, and/ or thirdly, drink. To bear not rising or falling but only continuing.

DICK: Just to bear it?

AMOS: What other?

DICK: *I* used to drink.

AMOS: You are drunk as you speak, sir. Drink to bear it and what?

DICK: To end up sooner.

AMOS: Soonest. Right. You know how much I love the boy?

DICK: Not enough?

AMOS: And right again. If you think you know how to live better, then do so. Take him far away.

DICK: Come on.

(DICK *holds a hand out to* TOMMY, *who doesn't move.*)

TOMMY: I won't tell you where she's gone.

DICK: It don't matter. Come on.

(*Still* TOMMY *won't move.*)

AMOS: How far away from a beatin' are you?

TOMMY: But you can't even stand.

(*With surprising speed and force,* AMOS *gets to his feet and takes one step toward* TOMMY.)

(TOMMY *steps closer to* DICK *and* NORBERT, *then stops.*)

DICK: Norbert?

(DICK *nods at the monkey, who looks at him and then crosses to* TOMMY.)

(NORBERT *holds out his paw.*)

(TOMMY *considers, then takes the monkey's paw, and follows* DICK *off.*)

(AMOS *is left alone in the hall.*)

AMOS: "The golf links are so near the mill
that almost every day,
the laboring children can look out..."
(*He looks off.*) Tommy?

(*The lights fade to black.*)

Scene Six

(DICK's room)

(A narrow bed and a chair)

*(*NORBERT *and* TOMMY *lie side by side on the bed, asleep, the covers knocked off.*

*(*DICK *sleeps sitting up in a chair, nearby.)*

(Suddenly, there's a very loud knock on the door.)

MRS LANE: *(Off)* Mister Hunter!

*(*DICK *struggles awake.)*

DICK: PRESENT!

MRS LANE: *(Off)* Please to forgo the fripperies, sir. I am using my master key instanter. Make yourself as decent as lies within your admittedly limited power.

*(*DICK *stands up, sees* NORBERT *and* TOMMY, *and does a double take.)*

DICK: Norbert, old bean! And Tommy. Oh, no…

*(*DICK *grabs a sheet and wafts it over* NORBERT *and* TOMMY, *just as* MRS LANE *enters.)*

MRS LANE: I smell urchin odor.

DICK: Last week you were smelling orangutans, madam—

MRS LANE: Don't look at my nose in that clearly satirical fashion—

DICK: I only suggest that a doctor's attention—

MRS LANE: Then what is *that*? *(She points past him to the bumps beneath the sheet.)*

(Before DICK *can stop her,* MRS LANE *yanks the sheet off.* NORBERT *and* TOMMY *sleep on.)*

MRS LANE: A human child and a chimpanzee. In your bed. This doesn't look good. You aren't a Uranian, are you, sir?

DICK: I could try to explain....

MRS LANE: It would make my teeth hurt if you did. I can guess: the boy was being abused—

DICK: He was.

MRS LANE: And when all my rooms are full to bursting with limbless children and dogs with arthritis—where do you want *I* should live?

DICK: I'll move.

MRS LANE: Tonight.

(Pause)

DICK: If I settle with you, I won't have a thin dime. Or a thick one, either.

MRS LANE: I'm sorry to hear it.

DICK: I lost my job.

MRS LANE: And your breath would ignite if I lit a match. Are you certain it's fit to take on a small child at this point in your downward glide?

(MRS LANE *sits down on the side of the bed. Gently, she brushes* TOMMY's *hair with her hand—then suddenly stops herself.)*

DICK: No—touch him. His name is Tommy.

(MRS LANE *strokes* TOMMY's *hair again.)*

MRS LANE: Do you do this?

DICK: No. I'm afraid of him.

MRS LANE: Why?

DICK: We're rivals.

MRS LANE: Oh?

DICK: For a woman's affections. I think he loves her better than I do. He wants to protect her.

MRS LANE: And does he?

DICK: Yes. He won't tell me where she lives.

MRS LANE: And her name is—

DICK: Susan.

MRS LANE: The one in the photo you showed me.

DICK: Yes.

MRS LANE: "Very late at night you get lonely," you said.

DICK: Don't you?

(MRS LANE *continues to soothe* TOMMY.)

MRS LANE: *(Very soft)* Tommy.

TOMMY: *(Asleep)* Uhn…

MRS LANE: Are you dreaming?

TOMMY: Umf…

MRS LANE: It's Susan.

(DICK *is startled.* TOMMY *sighs.*)

MRS LANE: I miss you.

DICK: Look: He's started to cry in his sleep. Better stop…

MRS LANE: Don't cry. I want you to come and see me. Will you?

TOMMY: Susan…

(Pause)

MRS LANE: Do you know where I live?

TOMMY: Ain't mulberries trees? You see any trees in this pigpen?

DICK: Mulberries?

MRS LANE: *(To* DICK*)* Mulberry Bend. Downtown. *(She gets up from the bed. There are tears in her eyes.)*

DICK: Don't cry. Please don't.

MRS LANE: I give you one hour to load your circus. And then I will call the police. *(She goes to the door.)*

DICK: Why did you help me at all?

MRS LANE: I get lonely, late at night, like a stab in the heart—

DICK: Then let us stay on.

MRS LANE: —but I hold my breath, long enough, and the pain goes away.

*(*MRS LANE *exits.* DICK *looks at the boy and the chimp, as the lights fade out.)*

Scene Seven

(A five-cent lodging house, like the one DICK *took a picture of at the top of the play.)*

(People sleep on cots, on the floor, on boxes, on top of each other.)

(The room is briefly lit as the hall door opens. DICK *comes in, with* TOMMY *asleep in his arms.* NORBERT *brings up the rear; he carries* DICK's *bag.)*

(With difficulty, DICK *and* NORBERT *step over the sleeping bodies trying to find a clear space to sleep.)*

SLEEPING MAN ONE: What the fuck—

DICK: Sorry.

SLEEPING MAN TWO: Yer foot's in my face, dumb asshole—

DICK: Excuse me.

SLEEPING MAN THREE: Hey! I smell monkey!

SLEEPING MAN ONE: Ya smell your own crack.

SLEEPING MAN TWO: Go to sleep!

SLEEPING MAN THREE: Oh, bite it off, ham-fat.

SLEEPING MAN TWO: SLEEP!

(DICK *finally finds a tiny space, and awkwardly sets down* TOMMY, *who wakes.*)

TOMMY: You took me home.

DICK: It's another place.

TOMMY: It smells worse.

DICK: You were used to the other, that's all.

TOMMY: It smells worse.

(DICK *and* NORBERT *squeeze into the space on the floor beside* TOMMY.)

DICK: Here: Put your head in my lap.

TOMMY: No, thanks. *(He curls up in a tight little ball on the floor.)* Don't you have friends?

DICK: Not many, lately.

TOMMY: You broke?

DICK: I had fifteen cents. That bought us three spots on the floor.

(Pause)

TOMMY: What happens tomorrow?

DICK: I find her.

TOMMY: How? You don't know where she lives.

DICK: Don't you want to find her?

TOMMY: I want you to leave us alone. *(Pause)* Did you fuck her? *(Pause)* Was she good? *(Pause)* Would you marry her? *(Pause)* You just want to fuck her again.

(DICK *grabs* TOMMY *up off the floor.*)

DICK: Shut UP!

TOMMY: Go on, hit me. *(Pause)* You nellie.

(DICK eases TOMMY back to the floor.)

DICK: I'm sorry, I—I'm sorry.

TOMMY: My old man can hit harder than you. *(Pause)*
But that's about all the difference. And your booze
costs more than his beer. *(Pause)* I wish you had left us
alone. *(He curls back up again.)*

(DICK reaches out a hand to touch him but can't quite do it.)

*(Near DICK, a man sitting up on the floor lights a pipe. We
see by the light of the match it's the MAN who called himself
Jack the Ripper. He's been listening to DICK and TOMMY.)*

(DICK smells the smoke and looks at the glow, uneasy.)

DICK: Isn't this place a fire-trap?

MAN: Who'd miss us?

(DICK can't answer. The MAN offers his pipe.)

MAN: Smells like burning rope, I know, but you're
welcome to take a pull….

DICK: No thanks.

(Pause)

MAN: That your boy?

DICK: No.

(Pause)

MAN: Were you ever that young?

DICK: I don't remember.

(Pause)

MAN: What'll happen to him?

DICK: I don't know.

(Pause)

MAN: I was as young as that. A long time ago. *(Pause)* I wish my father had snapped my neck.

DICK: Do you?

MAN: I wish he had.

(Unsettled, DICK turns back to TOMMY and strokes his hair.)

(In the dark, the MAN smokes his pipe and watches DICK.)

(The lights fade to black.)

Scene Eight

(A rooftop over the new bordello, where SUSAN is hiding out)

(Dusk)

(Lines of laundry flap in the breeze.)

(SUSAN stands at the edge of the roof, looking out at the city.)

ANNIE: *(Off)* Anybody to home in this heat? Hello? They said come up and rehearse…

(SUSAN turns, recognizing the voice.)

SUSAN: Annie?

ANNIE: *(Off)* Who in Hoboken is that? *(She comes around a flapping sheet and sees SUSAN.)* Susan!

(Delighted, ANNIE and SUSAN rush at each other and hug. ANNIE starts to sniffle.)

SUSAN: Don't.

ANNIE: Well, let me. We're sentimental, whores.

SUSAN: I know for a fact.

ANNIE: Mean as ferrets but sentimental. I thought we had certainly lost you.

SUSAN: My hope was that.

ANNIE: But I don't mean lost-*misplaced*, you whore. Lost like you even remember your hymen? Gone for gone. Old Halliwell down at the station said they just pulled a floater out of the river that maybe was you.

SUSAN: Why are *you* here?

ANNIE: Our old friend Madame Clafouti was rousted, is why. Two nights ago. I was out on my ass. I looked around. This circus was all I could find. It was this or the street.

SUSAN: What do you think about animal acts?

ANNIE: I guess if they're tastefully done…

SUSAN: Why was she rousted? Wasn't she paying the cops enough boodle?

ANNIE: Some of the bulls've been rousted too. Purity rearing its ugly head.

SUSAN: Purity…

(ANNIE *and* SUSAN *spit.*)

ANNIE: Be nice when things die down again.

SUSAN: I'd like to believe they always do.

ANNIE: Just, how many lambs do they have to make mutton before?

SUSAN: And speaking of which…

ANNIE: It's a lamb act?

SUSAN: No. It's a donkey.

ANNIE: Maybe I've made a mistake.

SUSAN: A small donkey.

ANNIE: Size wouldn't be my objection, so much.

SUSAN: Yes, it would.

(*Pause*)

ANNIE: Who'd want to watch?

SUSAN: Unhappy men.

ANNIE: Unhappy donkeys…where's our fellow thespian, then?

SUSAN: They let him sleep all day. He gathers his strength. We can practice without.

ANNIE: I'm game.

SUSAN: All right, then. *(She points to one of the sheets.)* Here's our curtain—

ANNIE: We get a curtain?

SUSAN: Exactly this. It's a sheet they hang in the parlor. We make a living tableau behind it, and freeze…and then you wait for the curtain to pull…and you're only a foot away, so you hear them…talking and laughing, and hoping it ever could be quite as good as they see, in their dim mind's eye…you can smell them, even, the ones that bathe and the ones that don't, and all of them greasing over a little with panic, because they are all— only few of them know it—afraid…

ANNIE: Of us?

SUSAN: Of what they wanted to see. Which I think is bodies behaving as if there was no death. And why they wanted to see it—because they are all of them going to die.

(Pause)

(ANNIE prompts.)

ANNIE: So we make a tableau…

SUSAN: And classical themes seem always to please. "The destruction of Carthage," how does that sound? You can be Conqueror Rome, and ride the donkey—

ANNIE: The animal's here? *(She pets an invisible donkey.)*

SUSAN: And I'll be Carthage down below in the dirt, being sacked. *(She sits on the roof and lies back.)*

ANNIE: Sacked in what manner?

SUSAN: Blowing the donkey.

(Pause)

ANNIE: Why would you do this, Susan?

SUSAN: Where else can I go? *(Pause)* I think I have come to the very far edge of the earth.

ANNIE: What are you running away from?

SUSAN: Nailing the donkey's hat to the ceiling. Facing up.

ANNIE: To what?

SUSAN: What I saw one night.

ANNIE: When?

SUSAN: Back in Chicago. Another life. At a rally. *(Pause)* For the eight-hour day...

ANNIE: What did you see?

(SUSAN doesn't respond.)

ANNIE: I'm as gone as you are. Tell.

(Pause)

SUSAN: I was on my way home. I was taking a shortcut. Across the square. The crowd was already drifting away, it was starting to rain. But I hadn't eaten all day, so I stopped to buy a damn bag of peanuts. I had my hand out for my change, but the man looked past me. His eyes had gone big. I turned and I saw this line of blue uniforms sweeping down. People were already running past me. I thought if, maybe instead of running, I moved ahead—the way the cops were coming, but off to the side—I'd be safe. So I started out...

ANNIE: And what did you see?

SUSAN: Well, most of the cops had already passed,
by then, I was edging along the side of the square,
and people were being trampled, and clubbed, but I
wouldn't look back, I kept moving ahead, I was almost
home and free…and I then I looked up and I saw a
copper pull a piece of lead pipe from under his tunic.
And then he turned to the man beside him, who lit the
fuse. And then the one with the pipe rushed forward
and tossed the bomb high up in the air. And then the
one who had lit the fuse looked off to the side and saw
me.

(Pause)

ANNIE: Are you sure that's what you saw?

SUSAN: Maybe not. The square was dark, and the rain
was falling harder. Maybe it only looked like a copper.
Maybe my life only looks like a rat-hole. Maybe it only
seems like I blow the damn donkey. Maybe I only blow
into the donkey. Maybe I use his dick for a nozzle.
Maybe I flood him with air, and he starts to swell up,
all over now, and finally lifts away from the floor…

ANNIE: Am I riding him still?

SUSAN: You are. Bareback, bare all your skin, and you
reach down just in time to pull me up too—

ANNIE: I think I'm happy. I'm happy?

SUSAN: Yes.

ANNIE: Are we aerial whores?

SUSAN: We're soaring broads, we're hot-air sluts, all
our juices are raining down—

ANNIE: Are we bumping the ceiling?

SUSAN: One bump and the plaster is flaking away, and
we're floating up into the night—

ANNIE: And the men are still watching?

SUSAN: The men have seen diddle. The men are still waiting for someone to open the curtain. We're higher, now. In fact, we're too high—

ANNIE: But we're happy.

SUSAN: Oh, yes. We don't stop being happy. Even the donkey is happy. And bigger. And bigger and bigger and bigger and finally— *(She grabs hold of the "curtain" sheet and yanks it aside.)*

(DICK and NORBERT are standing, surprised, on the other side.)

DICK: Bang.

SUSAN: You…

DICK: And then what happens?

ANNIE: And then it rains us and dead donkey for quite some time. *(To NORBERT)* You a customer, Jack? Or part of the acting ensemble?

DICK: He's with me.

ANNIE: That don't answer my question.

(Farther back on the roof, the MAN appears, disguised with a fake goatee and a blind man's round dark glasses and cane.)

SUSAN: How long were you there?

(DICK is embarrassed.)

SUSAN: How much did you hear?

DICK: I was waiting to find the right place. To interrupt—…

(SUSAN starts to run, DICK grabs her.)

DICK: I paid up for the night. From now to dawn.

(SUSAN jerks her hand away but doesn't flee. She looks at the MAN, who's tapping his way a bit closer.)

SUSAN: Who's your friend?

DICK: He was stumbling up the stairs just now. Another unsatisfied customer—

ANNIE: Heavens! Allow us a *moment*, please.

DICK: *(Pulling* SUSAN *off)* Come on. We have to talk.

SUSAN: *(Resisting)* You paid for sex. That's all you get. You can't afford my conversation.

DICK: Fine. Come on. We have to fuck. I'll take what I can get.

(Escorting SUSAN *through the maze of laundry,* DICK *leads her off.)*

MAN: *(Looking blindly around)* Is anyone left?

ANNIE: Over here.

(The MAN *taps his way to* ANNIE, *who takes his arm.)*

ANNIE: Myself, I think, if you want to talk all over me, talk. It's all the same to me.

MAN: I don't have to talk.

(The MAN *stares at her.* ANNIE *grows uncomfortable.)*

ANNIE: Nice night.

MAN: Is it?

ANNIE: Look. Oh… Well, it's nice. The moon's this little fingernail…

MAN: But listen.

ANNIE: What?

MAN: People suffering. Hear?

ANNIE: I guess, you grow up by the ocean, you don't hear surf.

(The MAN *continues to stare.)*

ANNIE: Did I eat too many onions and not enough Sensen, or what's your particular problem?

MAN: I wanted the other woman.

ANNIE: Even the blind man picks me second? That just about does it.

(Angrily, ANNIE starts to exit. The MAN grabs her hand.)

MAN: But don't you know you'll do?

(The lights fade out.)

Scene Nine

(SUSAN's new room)

(SUSAN enters, almost running, and starts to unbutton her gown. DICK hurries in after her.)

DICK: I want you to know. I ain't mad.

SUSAN: At what?

DICK: You hit me with a champagne bottle.

SUSAN: Not hard enough. And I guess you've bought the right to make me pay.

(DICK puts a hand on SUSAN's arm.)

DICK: You don't have to undress.

SUSAN: Hear that sandy falling sound? *(She pulls away.)*

DICK: I do. Have you ever been to the end of Long Island?

SUSAN: One, I'm not talking to you in the slightest. And two, you ain't combing my hair.

DICK: We don't have to—

SUSAN: Don't say it. FUCK? No shit, my shining knight. We don't never have ever to fuck you gents. It's low on your list, after coming, and being a few minutes petted and pampered, and first of all mainly a lot of chin music—

DICK: *(A question)* But coming ain't fucking.

SUSAN: Oh, sure it is. Like the second it takes to die out is your life.

DICK: I thought you weren't talking.

(Angrily she starts again to undress. He stops her.)

DICK: Tell me your name.

SUSAN: It's Ariadne.

DICK: The name you were born with.

SUSAN: "Naked"'s the name I was born with. So let me get down to it, now. *(She pulls away and continues undressing.)*

DICK: Your name is Susan.

(SUSAN's startled, but tries to hide it.)

DICK: My name is Dick.

SUSAN: Why don't that surprise.

DICK: And I've missed you, since last I saw you.

SUSAN: Invest in a dog.

DICK: I already own a hard-bitten monkey. I also adopted a boy.

SUSAN: One might guess you were lacking in inner resources.

DICK: I am.

SUSAN: Oh, no, you don't. Don't get all honest and wet with me—

DICK: You know the boy. His name is Tommy.

(SUSAN is startled.)

SUSAN: Adopted him?

DICK: Well, took him, I guess.

SUSAN: That sounds more like the way you work.

DICK: And he hates me.

SUSAN: He isn't dumb.

DICK: I watched him sleep all night, last night. He dreamt about you. He muttered your name. And you must have let him love you, I thought. And I hoped you might ever let me.

SUSAN: Is it my body you want? Or my story?

DICK: It's like they had almost become the same thing.

SUSAN: Then let's get down to the part that humps. You heard what you came to hear. Behind the sheet.

DICK: A policeman threw the bomb.

SUSAN: Yes.

DICK: That's quite a story.

SUSAN: Well, now you got it. Now you can use it to sell a few papers. The man who threw the bomb can find me and finish me off. And the innocent men who were hanged in his stead will be dead as they ever have been....

DICK: And you try to tell yourself, late at night—

SUSAN: Nothing. I tell myself nothing.

DICK: "I would have saved them if I could."

SUSAN: How the hell would you know.

DICK: I thought that about you. When I'd lost you. (*Pause*) You know the judge was prejudiced. And the jury was rigged. They'd have hooted you off the stand.

SUSAN: I guess. It don't help a whole lot.

DICK: So you offer yourself to a donkey.

(*She doesn't respond.*)

DICK: I drank. (*Pause*) My skin was sallow. My liver was swelling. My work had caromed galley-west. I used to ride out on the steam-cars, all the way to the end of Long Island, stagger down to the beach at night...stare off into the black pitch air and the roar and try to see the lights of Europe.

SUSAN: Could you?

DICK: Too far off. Land's end and open water. The wind shifts, and the sand piles up and blows away. Hear that "shoosh?" *(Pause)* And then I met you.

(Pause)

SUSAN: Would you bury my story forever?

DICK: If that's what you asked me to do.

SUSAN: I am only a body.

DICK: That's all I want, now.

SUSAN: Then look at me.

(DICK *turns to face* SUSAN'*s nakedness.*)

SUSAN: I can only fuck you.

DICK: That's all I...

SUSAN: And even you know you're too far gone to feel a thing.

DICK: I felt you, though. When I was inside. I felt the grain, like somebody saying...

SUSAN: Like nobody saying anything. Please. As the parts of my body don't speak in tongues. The grain of my cunt is only the grain of my cunt.

DICK: Like somebody saying, "Stay here".

SUSAN: *(A question)* Forever.

DICK: Just, "Stay. Move around a little. Stay. Hold tight. Feel. Something. Feel a part of someone. Stay."

(SUSAN *touches* DICK'*s face.*)

SUSAN: You'd have saved me if you could.

DICK: Not "would have." *Will.*

SUSAN: I'm diseased.

DICK: I don't care. I've had the clap myself—

SUSAN: It ain't clap. It's the other. The one that carries you off.

(DICK *takes this in.*)

DICK: Then maybe I have it myself, by now. *(Pause)* It don't matter—

SUSAN: It matters.

DICK: They're closing in on a cure—

SUSAN: —for umpteen years.

DICK: We could live a long time.

SUSAN: Or not.

(Pause)

DICK: Marry me.

(Pause)

(SUSAN *laughs.*)

SUSAN: Marry you. *(Pause)* All right. I'm honored. I guess I accept. What did you say your name was, again? *(She laughs some more.)*

DICK: Richard.

SUSAN: No, you said "Dick"—

DICK: Richard Hunter.

SUSAN: Mrs Dick Hunter. It has a ring—

DICK: I love you.

(Pause)

SUSAN: Then why'd a policeman kill policemen? To get to the other side. Why? I couldn't marry a man what didn't know.

DICK: Because the policeman's afraid.

SUSAN: Of what?

DICK: Of losing the little he has.

SUSAN: Who wants the policeman to be afraid? Of his fellow working man?

DICK: The owners.

SUSAN: So afraid that he's willing to martyr himself. So afraid that he's happy to martyr himself.

DICK: The owners.

SUSAN: Who do you work for, Dick?

DICK: Nobody. I'm fired.

SUSAN: Why?

DICK: I wanted to save you.

(Pause)

SUSAN: A doctor inspected me. Right before you fucked me, Dick. I was clean. Burned out, I mean. And now I'm not. *(Pause)* I was clean. And now I'm not.

DICK: *I* infected *you*?

SUSAN: And see how much that never once ever occurred?

(Pause)

DICK: I can't save you.

SUSAN: No.

DICK: I never could. You have to save yourself.

SUSAN: It's too late. The cop from Chicago is here. In the city. Down a dark alley. I feel him.

DICK: Do you?

SUSAN: You wanted to know why I was shaking. I feel him. Like a bad blood-fever. Look at my hands.

(DICK takes one of her hands in his.)

SUSAN: Now yours are trembling too.

DICK: What does he look like?

SUSAN: The glare of the bomb was behind him. I never saw his face.

DICK: Then he doesn't need to kill you.

SUSAN: I'll tell him that.

DICK: How will he find you?

SUSAN: It couldn't be that knotty a problem—*you* found me, Dick.

DICK: When will he show?

SUSAN: When I've given up waiting, I guess. And gone on with my life. And I'm hurrying down a dark alley, some night. And one of the shadows moves. And takes my hand.

(Pause)

DICK: Do you *like* to fuck the donkey?

(SUSAN slaps him.)

DICK: You have to save *yourself*.

SUSAN: HOW?

DICK: I don't know how. Walking down the aisle with me was the last clear thought I had.

(Pause)

(SUSAN starts to think of something.)

SUSAN: Take a picture.

DICK: What sort of picture?

SUSAN: Me. In a beautiful wedding gown. I wonder if they come in red.

DICK: *(Catching on)* Announcing a marriage.

SUSAN: Yours and mine…

DICK: Smoke him out of the shadows…

SUSAN: You think it could work? It could work….

DICK: I'd love to see you in a wedding gown.

SUSAN: But we only make believe…

DICK: If you want. Or we tie the knot for true.

SUSAN: Best make believe.

(The lights fade to black.)

Scene Ten

(Back on the roof of SUSAN's *bordello)*

(Night)

(One of the hanging sheets is splashed with blood. It drags along the ground.)

*(*NORBERT *steps out of the shadows, approaches the sheet)*

(He's very nervous, as if he'd been frightened by something.)

(Gingerly, he pulls the sheet back, like a curtain, revealing ANNIE *lying on her back, on the roof. Her wrists have been slashed.)*

*(*NORBERT *sits beside* ANNIE. *He stares at her, as if he were waiting to see her move. Then he looks out into the night.)*

(The lights fade to black.)

Scene Eleven

*(*BUNNER's *photography studio. A dropcloth, painted to look like woods, in back)*

*(*DICK, *dressed up to the bridegroom's nines, is pacing as* BUNNER—*ever unkempt—sets up his great big camera.)*

BUNNER: Let's see if I got this straight, at last: I take a picture of you and your doxy—

DICK: Her name is Susan.

BUNNER: —your doxy Susan, *as if* you was gonna get hitched, like your common or garden beloveds might, except you ain't gonna get married at all, you're only running another picture of mine. In a free and peculiar way.

DICK: To lure a killer out.

BUNNER: Which, as intentions go, is so worthy I guess I don't get to object that you're using me. One more time. *(He calls out)* HELLO!

SUSAN: *(Off, from behind the drop cloth)* I'm not quite ready—

BUNNER: Don't matter, my dear, the light's gone bad. Come out.

(BUNNER faces DICK off.)

DICK: You aren't serious.

BUNNER: Not ever more.

(SUSAN enters, dressed in a beautiful wedding gown, the back of which is unbuttoned.)

SUSAN: So many doors and rooms back there, I almost got lost. What's wrong?

DICK: He has an objection to taking the picture.

SUSAN: Why? *(To DICK)* Would you do my buttons up?

DICK: There's no need.

SUSAN: Oh, I'll take it right off, I just wanted to see myself, once. It's a beautiful dress.

BUNNER: It belonged to my wife. Your dress and his suit is a package deal. I lend it to out-of-pocket couples.

SUSAN: Well, that would be us to a T, all right.

(DICK fumbles with the buttons.)

SUSAN: What *are* your qualms?

DICK: If his photo suggests we're about to be married, he thinks we should honestly marry. And keep his work true. Which of course is exactly what I would like. You look, in that dress, most properly lovely. I very much wish this was real.

BUNNER: Why ain't it?

SUSAN: Well, to begin, we're both poxed up.

BUNNER: So die in each other's arms, why don't you.

SUSAN: And then there's the fact, I'm a whore.

BUNNER: So was my wife, it turned out, and it didn't stop us.

SUSAN: Won't you let us pretend?

BUNNER: I won't go along. No.

DICK: We're trying to save this woman's life.

BUNNER: And how'd you put it in jeopardy?

(Pause)

DICK: I ran a photo of yours.

BUNNER: That's right.

(Pause)

SUSAN: Apologize, Dick.

DICK: I'm sorry.

(Pause)

BUNNER: If I *was* gonna take your picture, now—and it still looks dicey, honest to god—I'd ask you to stand over there. In front of those woods.

(DICK and SUSAN move in front of the forest dropcloth.)

DICK: These woods are a lie.

BUNNER: Those woods are true. True paint on cloth. That's all I say they are.

(As DICK *and* SUSAN *hold hands,* TOMMY *and* NORBERT *enter.)*

*(*TOMMY*'s cleaned up and wearing new knickers.)*

BUNNER: What's this? A monkey walking his boy?

*(*SUSAN *comes down to fuss over* TOMMY*.)*

SUSAN: Look at you, Tommy! All spiffed up.

*(*TOMMY *squirms away.)*

TOMMY: I never saw *you* this clean your old self.

BUNNER: What's the occasion?

TOMMY: *(Nodding at* DICK*)* He got me a job at the paper.

BUNNER: *(To* DICK*)* I thought you was fired.

DICK: Another paper.

BUNNER: They take *you* on?

DICK: They're considerin'…

BUNNER: I guess it would be quite a scoop. If you caught this man.

DICK: I guess it would.

(Pause)

BUNNER: So scamper back into the woods, you two…

*(*NORBERT *and* TOMMY *start to join the adults, and* BUNNER *shoos them back.)*

BUNNER: …and *you* two stand aside for now, this here is a wedding engagement photo, they ain't supposed to have had the kid and the monkey yet.

*(*DICK *and* SUSAN *stand, arm in arm, in front of the painted trees.)*

BUNNER: You want a job, son?

TOMMY: I guess.

BUNNER: All right. Now if Darwin here can hold the pan—

TOMMY: His name is Norbert.

BUNNER: Whatever. Norbert.

(BUNNER *hands* NORBERT *the frying pan full of powder, and then he gives* TOMMY *the starter pistol.*)

BUNNER: You shoot right into this pan when I give you the word. That clear?

TOMMY: I'm *small*. I'm not *dumb*.

(BUNNER *gets under the drop cloth, as* NORBERT *holds up the powder pan and* TOMMY *prepares to shoot the pistol.*)

BUNNER: And you lovebirds look at each other like this was the genuine article.

(DICK *and* SUSAN *turn and look at each other. He touches her face.*)

TOMMY: Take the picture, fer cryin' out loud.

BUNNER: On a count of three: One…two…

(*At that moment,* NORBERT *suddenly tenses. He sniffs the air with such alarm that his tail shoots up. He follows the scent he's picked up to the dropcloth. He sniffs the painted trees.*)

DICK: Feelin' homesick, fellah?

BUNNER: Could we get the chimp back to the firing line?

(NORBERT *looks behind the drop cloth.*)

(*Then he screams a horrible scream and starts running from* DICK *to* BUNNER *and back.*)

BUNNER: Ain't it hard to find decent help these days? Norbert, heel!

(*But* NORBERT *won't stop running around.*)

DICK: Norbert?

(NORBERT *suddenly stops and stares at the drop cloth.*)

(*A straight razor, making a horrible ripping sound, rips into the painted trees, from top to bottom.*)

(*The* MAN *steps through the slit he's made and grabs* SUSAN, *holding the razor against her neck.*)

MAN: Step back, every single one.

(BUNNER, DICK, NORBERT *and* TOMMY *move back, all staring at* SUSAN.)

MAN: And you tell them.

SUSAN: What?

MAN: You were waiting for this.

SUSAN: Where were you hiding?

MAN: In one of the rooms in back. I broke in last night. I was waiting for this. So were you.

SUSAN: I used to be waiting. Yes.

MAN: And this is our wedding day.

SUSAN: No, it ain't. It's not.

(*With his free hand, the* MAN *pulls a yellowed piece of newsprint out of his pocket and thrusts it in* SUSAN's *trembling fingers.*)

MAN: Read it.

SUSAN: I can't—

MAN: READ IT.

SUSAN: I can't. I can't hold it still.

DICK: May I?

(*Pause*)

(*The* MAN *stares at* DICK, *then he grabs the paper from* SUSAN *and flings it at* DICK, *who picks it up and reads.*)

DICK: "Dynamite. Of all the good stuff—"

MAN: Read it as if you meant it! Read it as if you wrote it!

DICK: An anarchist wrote it. I heard this once at the trial.

MAN: *You* wrote it. You stood at the head of the rickety table, carving the pitiful roast, and you looked at your worn-away wife and children, and felt how sharp the knife in your hand, and how keen their trust, and they held their plates for the little you had to give, and you thought, "I could cut their throats like butter. I COULD CUT THEIR THROATS LIKE BUTTER!"

DICK: Why?

MAN: Because how could I hope to save them? READ!

DICK: *(Reading, louder)* "DYNAMITE! Of all the good stuff, this is the stuff. Stuff several pounds of this sublime stuff into an inch pipe, gas or water—"

(The MAN joins in, reciting from heart.)

DICK & MAN: *(Loud)* "—plug up both ends, insert a cap with fuse attached, place this in the immediate neighborhood of a lot of rich loafers who live by the sweat of other people's brows, and light the fuse. A most cheerful and gratifying result will follow."

(Pause)

DICK: And your family. *Did* you save them?

MAN: They'd already left me. Long before.

DICK: And the children of all the people you killed?

MAN: It was for them I died.

DICK: You didn't die.

(Pause)

MAN: I did. *(To* SUSAN*)* And you did too. We're married already.

(SUSAN *doesn't deny it.*)

MAN: The bomb went off—

SUSAN: *You* lit the fuse. I only watched you do it.

MAN: And people were hanged. For what I did. Did you watch that, too? *(Pause)* DID YOU WATCH THAT, TOO?

(Pause)

SUSAN: I would have saved them if I could.

MAN: But you didn't. Did you?

SUSAN: No.

MAN: Then marry me.

(Pause)

SUSAN: All right.

DICK: Tommy, shoot!

(TOMMY *aims at the* MAN *and fires. A small explosion, but nothing happens. The* MAN *is unharmed.*)

BUNNER: *(Whispered)* It's a starter-pistol, kid! You're firing blanks! Shoot into the pan!

TOMMY: Norbert!

(*As* NORBERT *runs over,* TOMMY *fires the pistol into the frying-pan, and the room lights up in the frozen suspended glare.*)

(*The* MAN *holds the razor up to his eyes to block the light.*)

(DICK *lunges forward and grabs the* MAN's *hand. Their fight for the razor holds it unmoving, up in the air. Then, with a surge of panic-strength, The* MAN *overpowers* DICK, *badly slashing his hand.*)

(DICK *gasps and falls to his knees. The* MAN *grabs* SUSAN *again.*)

(BUNNER *starts to move to help* DICK, *but the* MAN *holds him back with the bloody razor.* TOMMY *and* NORBERT *gape.*)

MAN: Didn't I die? *(Pause)* DIDN'T I DIE? *(Pause)* I lit the fuse. The pipe went up. I had just a few seconds to place myself. I wanted the bomb to be right above me. I wanted to see the light break out. All around.

DICK: But you didn't get under the bomb.

MAN: I froze.

DICK: Why?

(*The* MAN *faces* SUSAN, *pulling her close. He speaks to her.*)

MAN: Because I saw you.

(*No one dares to move—except* NORBERT, *who edges up with the frying pan.*)

MAN: I saw you. Looking at me. *(Pause)* You weren't frightened.

SUSAN: No.

MAN: Or shocked.

SUSAN: No.

MAN: You were *sad. (Pause)* You were PITYING ME. Raise your head. Hold it high as you held it that night. *My* head is high. I don't need to be pitied. Look at me one more time.

(*The* MAN *lifts the razor high up in the air;* SUSAN *exposes her throat*)

(*At that moment* NORBERT *strikes, conking the* MAN *with the frying pan. The* MAN *staggers, dropping the razor. Coolly,* NORBERT *conks him again. The* MAN *sinks to his knees.* NORBERT *whacks him again. The* MAN *pitches forward onto his face.* NORBERT *briefly examines the* MAN. *Then he starts to hit him again with the pan—over and over and over.*)

DICK: *(Wary)* Norbert?

(But NORBERT *won't stop.)*

BUNNER: I reckon he's gotten the message, sport.

*(*NORBERT *continues to whack the unconscious man, with rising fury.)*

(Uneasy at first, the spectators are now appalled.)

*(*DICK *approaches* NORBERT, *tapping him on the shoulder.)*

*(*NORBERT *wheels, turns to face* DICK, *and then—he screams: a single blood-curdling scream.* DICK *gently pries the frying pan from the monkey's grip. Then he gestures to* TOMMY, *who comes and takes the panting monkey off to one side.* TOMMY *gravely tries to cool the monkey down.)*

*(*DICK *feels the* MAN *for a pulse.* BUNNER *gives him a look;* DICK *shakes his head.)*

*(*BUNNER *picks* SUSAN's *wedding veil from the floor and hands it to* DICK, *who uses it to bind his bleeding hand.)*

(Then BUNNER *grabs the man by the arms and starts to drag him off.)*

BUNNER: How'd this happen again?

DICK: He fell downstairs.

*(*BUNNER *drags the* MAN *through the ripped-up backdrop of trees and exits.)*

*(*DICK *approaches Susan, who's far away.* TOMMY *and* NORBERT *draw closer.)*

DICK: He's gone, now.

SUSAN: No. He's not. I said I would marry him, Dick.

TOMMY: You were pulling his leg.

DICK: Marry *me.*

SUSAN: We were married already, he said. He was right.

DICK: You just got a divorce. He's gone now.

SUSAN: No, he's NOT.

DICK: Then he *will* be gone. He'll start to fade.

SUSAN: When?

DICK: When you marry me. And we stay awhile in each other's arms—

SUSAN: And maybe die in each other's arms—

DICK: Don't everyone die?

TOMMY: Who's dying?

DICK: Nobody you know.

SUSAN: Do you want him to love you?

DICK: Yes.

SUSAN: Don't start out with a lie.

(Pause)

DICK: Susan and I may have to leave you.

TOMMY: Soon?

DICK: I hope not.

TOMMY: When?

DICK: I don't know.

TOMMY: Don't say "leave me". I know the word.

DICK: We may die.

TOMMY: You almost died just now.

SUSAN: That's right.

TOMMY: And that could keep happenin', right? You could almost die, and almost die. And get old.

DICK: We could.

(SUSAN gives DICK a look.)

DICK: We could!

SUSAN: I don't see us old.

DICK: What *do* you see?

(SUSAN *doesn't answer.*)

DICK: I see you. You and Tommy, holding your hands up high to catch leaves—

TOMMY: What leaves?

DICK: In the Park. Not now but soon. This autumn. Out in the heat of this Indian summer—

TOMMY: Afternoon…

DICK: Late afternoon, you two'll be gassing away and I'll amble ahead, around a turn in the path and on into a clearing I never knew was there—

SUSAN: —and you'll be alone—

DICK: —in the sun, in a hidden meadow, and feel so lonely, for just a moment, I think my heart will break. And then I look back and I see you coming, you three, all chattering, laughing, hand in hand…and I think, "I have never been ever this happy before. In my life. With my wife and my son and my chimp. All alone. In a wood." *(Pause)* Can you see it? Even a little?

SUSAN: No. *(Pause)* But make me see.

(The lights fade to black.)

END OF PLAY

www.ingramcontent.com/pod-product-compliance
Lightning Source LLC
Chambersburg PA
CBHW052126090426
42741CB00009B/1964